Matchmaking in the Archive

Q+ Public books are a limited series of curated volumes, inspired by the seminal journal *OUT/LOOK: National Lesbian and Gay Quarterly*. *OUT/LOOK* built a bridge between academic inquiry and the broader community. Q+ Public promises to revitalize a queer public sphere to bring together activists, intellectuals, and artists to explore questions that urgently concern all LGBTQ+ communities.

Series editors: E. G. Crichton, Jeffrey Escoffier (from 2018–2022)

E. G. Crichton, *Matchmaking in the Archive: 19 Conversations with the Dead and 3 Encounters with Ghosts*
Shantel Gabriel Buggs and Trevor Hoppe, eds., *Unsafe Words: Queering Consent in the #MeToo Era*
Andrew Spieldenner and Jeffrey Escoffier, eds., *A Pill for Promiscuity: Gay Sex in an Age of Pharmaceuticals*

Matchmaking in the Archive

*19 Conversations with the Dead
and 3 Encounters with Ghosts*

E. G. CRICHTON

Rutgers University Press
New Brunswick, Camden, and Newark, New Jersey
London and Oxford, UK

Rutgers University Press is a department of Rutgers, The State University of New Jersey, one of the leading public research universities in the nation. By publishing worldwide, it furthers the University's mission of dedication to excellence in teaching, scholarship, research, and clinical care.

Library of Congress Cataloging-in-Publication Data
Names: Crichton, E. G., author.
Title: Matchmaking in the archive : 19 conversations with the
dead and 3 encounters with ghosts / E. G. Crichton.
Description: New Brunswick : Rutgers University Press, [2023] |
Series: Q+public | Includes bibliographical references and index.
Identifiers: LCCN 2022012372 | ISBN 9781978823136 (paperback) |
ISBN 9781978823143 (hardback) | ISBN 9781978823150 (epub) |
ISBN 9781978823174 (pdf)
Subjects: LCSH: Archives in art. | Sexual minorities in art. |
Dr. John P. De Cecco Archives and Research Center.
Classification: LCC CD971 .C75 2023 | DDC 306.76—dc23/eng/20220830
LC record available at https://lccn.loc.gov/2022012372

A British Cataloging-in-Publication record for this book is available
from the British Library.

rutgersuniversitypress.org

Manufactured in the United States of America

Dedicated to the nineteen individuals whose artifacts survived them, resisted erasure, and came back queerly in the works of nineteen living creators.

Contents

Series Foreword

Q+ Public is a series of small thematic books in which lead-ing scholars, artists, community leaders and activists, inde-pendent writers, and thinkers engage in critical reflection on contemporary LGBTQ political, social, and cultural issues.

Why Q+ Public? It invites all of the L, the G, the B, the T, the Q, and any other sexual and gender minorities. It asserts the need and existence of a queer public space. It is also a riff on "John Q. Public" stripped of his gender, and even on *Star Trek*'s "Q Continuum." Q+ Public is about elevating the challenges of thinking about gender, sex, and sexuality in contemporary life.

Q+ Public is an outgrowth, after a long hibernation, of *OUT/LOOK: National Lesbian and Gay Quarterly*, a pioneer-ing political and cultural journal that sparked intense national debate during the time it was published in San Fran-cisco, 1988–1992. *OUT/LOOK*, in turn, spawned the Out-Write conferences that started out in San Francisco in 1990 and 1991, then moved to Boston for a number of years.

We plan to revive *OUT/LOOK*'s political and cultural agenda in a new format. We aim to revitalize a queer public sphere in which to explore questions that urgently concern all LGBTQ communities. The movement that started with Stonewall was built on the struggles for political and civil rights of people of color, women, labor unions, and the disabled. These struggles led, unwittingly, to a major recon-figuration of the sex/gender system. The world of Stonewall was fading, and the new queer world was being born.

Our first books in this series address themes of queering consent, queer archive interventions, and whether PrEP (pre-exposure prophylaxis) is a pill for promiscuity. Each book finds a way to dive into the deep nuances and discomforts of each topic. Other books on the struggle for LGBTQ K–12 curriculum, the intersection of race and gender, and the incarceration of people with AIDS are in preparation.

We anticipate future volumes on shifting lesbian, queer, and trans identities; immigration, race, and homophobia; queer aging and the future of queer communities; new forms of community-based queer history; and LGBTQ politics after marriage, to name a few. Each book features multiple points of view, strong art, and a strong editorial concept.

In this era of new political dangers, Q+ Public takes on the challenges we face and offers a forum for public dialogue.

In *Matchmaking in the Archive: 19 Conversations with the Dead and 3 Encounters with Ghosts*, E. G. Crichton takes us on a captivating journey through the Gay Lesbian Bisexual Transgender Historical Society archives to get to know some of the individuals whose lives are represented there. Her methodology is to matchmake the archive of a dead individual to a living individual, asking the latter to invent a response. What unfolds on these pages are the relationships that emerge between the living and dead participants, and the resulting creative works.

E. G. Crichton
Jeffrey Escoffier

Preface

As a child, I collected stones and dipped them in water to bring out their colors. The smooth hard surfaces were soothing as I held them, one at a time, then arranged them just so beside my bed. As an adult, my collecting instinct more resembles that of a scavenger experiencing the thrill of the hunt, a recognition of potential, and pride in spotting the one item that stands out in a sea of junk. It reminds me of Walter Benjamin's ragpicker: "Here we have a man whose job it is to gather the day's refuse in the capital. Everything that the big city has thrown away, everything it has lost, everything it has scorned, everything it has crushed underfoot he catalogues and collects."[1] Rag picking is part of my art process, but even if I were not an artist, I would still be a scavenger.

Over the decades, I have sifted through a myriad of historical debris: old photographs, secondhand clothing, discarded letters, travel cases from the 1940s, vintage typewriters, broken rocking chairs—almost anything with the patina of age. I call myself a flea market junkie. It is a thrilling and addictive activity, and even more so the further I stray from home where ordinary objects appear more exotic. I am not a hoarder, but I do find it difficult to get rid of stuff. More than one friend has described my house as a museum.

My collecting desires are not unlike shopping, and the relationship to consumerism is undeniable. It is also true that going to a thrift store or garage sale will almost always lift my spirits. As I grow older, I wonder whether scavenging might be an attempt to stave off the inexorable march of time. I am driven by curiosity about the items that attract my attention, wondering who owned them, who discarded them, why they ended up where I found them. As I write, I look down at one example I collected sometime in the 1990s. It is a small sepia-toned photograph framed in a simply embossed gray cardboard mat. In it is pictured a cluster of five adults and five children. Most are wearing hats as they sit on the grass in front of a wide tree trunk. I am guessing it is a family cluster and their clothing suggests around 1900. At the exact center, framed symmetrically by the tree trunk, is a woman who appears powerful, more so than the adults seated further back to either side. Although faded, the photographic image is intact, with one exception. Two slashes cut across the woman's face to reveal the pulp of the paper on which the photograph is printed. I can feel the rough texture of these marks with my finger. They suggest a violent act, an intentional aggression across this woman's face that is so specifically targeted it cannot possibly be the random damage of time. More than any other object I have collected, this photograph continues to haunt me.

I recognize my fixation with this object as a strong desire to eavesdrop on the past. I yearn to know who disfigured this woman's facial identity and what went on in that family, if it was a family. The slashes that obliterate her features signal a secret I can't know, a clue to buried trauma, a repressed narrative I try to conjure. The delicate tissue of the secret always catches my attention, and in this case the exposure of paper pulp renders it literal. I experience something similar when—every few years—I drag out the boxes that contain remnants from the lives of my parents and one brother, all

dead. I wish I could ask each of them about the things that make no sense: Why did they save this, what is that for, who gave you this, what happened here? More secrets, and I realize secrets form the structure of much of my work. In crafting visual narratives from found fragments, I act as a kind of gatekeeper, reconstructing the milieu of the secret in material and ephemeral forms. This is my exploration of both memory and record, my way of spying on the dead.

These scavenging urges are what eventually led me to archives. Institutional archives, queer archives, archives I construct as I collect archaic knowledge, debunked theories, records of human prejudice, and the residue of querying my own life and family history. My family of origin is, after all, where I first encountered secrets and withheld information, mysteries I pondered as I held those small stones. Archives are where I spot gaps in a narrative, where what is absent calls out as loudly as what has been preserved. They are the site of a different form of scavenging, and this has been especially true in queer community archives like the Lesbian Herstory Archives in Brooklyn, the Leather Archives and Museum in Chicago, the June L. Mazer and the ONE archives in Los Angeles, and the Gay Lesbian Bisexual Transgender (GLBT) Historical Society in San Francisco. I have meandered many of their aisles without a specific goal, curious and alert, waiting for something or someone to call out. There is one crucial difference between these archives and my sites of scavenging for treasures: the objects in an archive are not for sale, not to be handled excessively, certainly not to be altered. The relationship to artifacts is more formal than in a library, where you can take books home for a period of time. The artifacts in an archive are generally one of a kind, not to be replicated, unique to a particular collecting institution.

Given the rules and order of archives, it is curious that I find the generally prosaic contents of their containers so inspiring. My drive toward archival research is palpable, yet very much in tension with a negotiation of the materials and forms that make up an artwork. This is the challenge of archive art: how to allow archive materials to inform a work while rendering them absent, unalterable, not illustratable in a literal way. Working in archives has taught me a kind of visual and aural translation that incorporates objects, images, and text, but also encourages the interdisciplinary mimicking of structures such as archive boxes, oral interviews, the recording of voice actors as they speak an archived person's words. More relevant to this book, archive research has encouraged me to invite collaboration and participation, to invent structures of interaction with historical materials that are generative, to find ways to bring an archive out of its temperature-controlled environment into public visibility through metaphors of art. The strategies and structures I develop to engage other people have become a creative form in itself, one I frame and test like a scientist.

Over the past two decades, I have developed a unique set of interdisciplinary art projects that find their roots in the queer historical memory reflected in archives. My methodology has centered on the performative act of matching a living individual to a deceased one, one archive organization to another, two deceased individuals in dialogue based on records of their words. To my usual art roles as maker in a studio, exhibition designer, academic researcher, detective in search of clues, or social scientist conducting an oral interview, I added a new role—matchmaker in the archive. For each project, I invent ways to attract collaborators who also become creative agents. My role is one part matchmaker, one part art director, one part maker, and one part medium to the dead.

In this book, I describe the first extended project I developed as artist-in-residence for the GLBT Historical Society, *LINEAGE: Matchmaking in the Archive*. The matchmaking that forms the core of this project has spawned a rich trove of dialogue, images, objects, writing, time-based media, and, above all, uncommon relationships. Underlying the creative work are questions I ask: What is our lineage? What is mine? How do we remember individual people after they die, and what does a person's archive reveal? And just as critical, what is absent from the archive, what secrets do the artifacts suggest, what shimmers in the gaps? It turns out that absence of information and suppressed histories provide incredibly fertile ground for artists to explore and imagine forms of lineage ordinarily invisible to the culture at large.

From 2008 through 2014, I spent countless day and nighttime hours at the GLBT Historical Society, perusing the catalog, meandering the aisles, pouring over boxes, and jotting down notes on each archive that caught my attention.

In contrast, the period of writing this book has dovetailed with the COVID-19 pandemic, a time when the archive has been off limits. As is often the case with limitations, this one spurred me to find other ways to search for new information and possibilities, to expand my knowledge of some of the archives I write about. At times, this has complicated the relationship between a living participant, their archive match, me, and a new living informant.

In this book, I translate the *LINEAGE* project to the written page as I talk about the process, about the living and the dead participants, and about the work we all created. I take up the challenge to push these art forms into a text that is read, looked at, and published. It is not unlike the way an archive distills a person's life into folders, files, and boxes—a tangible biography revealed through the artifacts that survive a person. I imagine this book as an index to an entire experience of thought, movement, the weaving of ideas through time. Each archive I write about suggests a unique narrative, one that is gathered and told and interpreted. The work of participants, the relationship between an archived person and a living person, gives that archive a body. Each box, each folder is filled with the possibility of touch, smell, sight, sound: the metaphorical taste of one person's life.

In both text and images, I describe each matched archive relationship and the creative work it spawned. In 2020, I invited three new participants to ponder their relationship to queer memory, queer ancestors, and notions of lineage. Jonathan D. Katz, Michelle Tea, and Chris E. Vargas have contributed essays that offer new perspectives on our relationship to our queer past.

Finally, I use the word "queer" throughout this book as an inclusive term, rather than a frequently shifting set of acronym letters. This is not meant to designate the specific identity labels used by the people about whom I write.

Matchmaking in the Archive

PART 1

Resurrection

One Life at a Time

The longing for community across time is a crucial feature
of queer historical experience, one produced by the
historical isolation of individual queers as well as by
the damaged quality of the historical archive.
—Heather Love, *Feeling Backward:*
Loss and the Politics of Queer History

This was not the first archive I lifted from an industrial gray
steel shelf that summer afternoon in 2008, but it was the most
manageable. As I carried the box like precious cargo to a
small table at the end of the aisle, I could feel its contents
shift with a brisk swishing sound. A quick glance toward the
archivist's desk reassured me she was not monitoring my little
disturbance, so I donned the wrinkled white gloves in preparation to touch.

I knew from a penciled label that the items inside the box
belonged to Lawrence DeCeasar, a.k.a. Larry Langtry.
Good, I had never heard of DeCeasar, never seen a display

of his objects, so he already fulfilled one of my criteria: Larry DeCeasar was not famous. Opening the lid, I was stunned by what I found inside. Instead of the tidy array of manila folders I had come to expect, this box held a jumble of more flashy items: silver sequined gloves carefully packaged in a plastic baggie, a neon pink embroidered satin vest, a small plastic box with what looked like costume brooches, and an aged baggie with bolero ties. A set of old black-and-white photo booth strips revealed the face of someone posing self-consciously at different stages of their life.

A small spread of loosely packed manila folders hugged one end of the box. There were no labels, but I could see handwritten song lyrics on torn cardboard and flimsy printed notices peeking out at odd angles, their order seemingly quite random. Some archive boxes I had been perusing held densely packed folders that were difficult to pry apart. I would often drag a stool to the shelf where these record-heavy boxes resided, in order to open lids and take a look without the heavy lifting. It was a relief that DeCeasar had only a single box, a light one in comparison, one with ephemera, which in archive lingo refers to clothing and other personal effects. Everything about this box was captivating and decidedly queer.

But who was DeCeasar beyond the glitter and charm of his artifacts? What would my relationship to this flamboyant gay performer from another era look like, and how could I delve deeper? I am, after all, an artist—not an archivist, historian, or journalist—an artist with a desire to excavate the dead, to reach out across the mortal threshold and speak to them. Hadn't I been tracking dead individuals and archaic expertise for years? Hadn't I been imagining conversations with the dead all along?

In that moment I had a very concrete question: Was DeCeasar dead? This would become one of my rules: the people whose archives I singled out had to be dead. I was learning that archives are quite a scattered, nonconforming enterprise; most of the ones I was looking at did not have a tidy index or a timeline, or even a date span like a tombstone. Sifting through a box to figure out if a person is alive or dead can be elusive, and twice in my archive art work I prematurely killed someone off, to some degree of embarrassment, by assuming that a friend or family member had donated a person's artifacts after that person's demise. But people who plan ahead—and I am not one of them—sometimes curate their own archive while alive. They sort through their stuff and decide what should go in a box, and what someone like me doing research in the archive will discover about them in the future.

The Archives, the 1980s, and AIDS

The archives I was poring over that summer are part of the collections housed at the Gay Lesbian Bisexual Transgender (GLBT) Historical Society in San Francisco. My connection to this organization began in the late 1970s while I was attending slide lectures given by people who started an important precursor organization: the San Francisco Lesbian and Gay History Project. I remember a riveting presentation in June 1979 by the historian Alan Bérubé called "Lesbian Masquerade: Some Lesbians in Early San Francisco Who Passed as Men." Bérubé had searched through San Francisco newspapers for local evidence of this phenomenon. Although very much constructed as a discovery of hidden lesbian lives, the presentation of "Lesbian Masquerade" also inspired explorations of transgender history.

The Gay and Lesbian Historical Society was founded in 1985 when a group of about sixty people met at the San

Francisco Public Library to discuss establishing an association to document and promote Bay Area queer history. Over the next few years, what had started as a collection of boxes crowded into one person's living room grew into a professionally managed archive of more than nine hundred collections. In 1999, the organization changed its name to GLBT Historical Society to acknowledge both trans and bisexual identities. The GLBT Historical Society is now an international leader in the field of queer history, with a large archive research site in midtown San Francisco and a small GLBT history museum in the Castro district, where the archives are curated into exhibitions and rendered visible to a larger public.

The historical milieu into which the GLBT Historical Society was born was the emergent AIDS crisis of the 1980s. Thousands of Bay Area gay men and some women were dying at relatively young ages, prematurely leaving behind the physical traces of their shortened lives. Out of this traumatic urgency, a movement of support and intervention like no other emerged across the country in the form of activist organizations such as ACT UP (AIDS Coalition to Unleash Power), Gay Men's Health Crisis, Gran Fury, and Lambda Legal Defense, along with networks of progressive healthcare professionals and women's groups. As groups with primarily white middle-class members confronted public fear and government and medical inaction, the racism of omission often neglected less entitled and more vulnerable populations inside and outside of queer communities—poor people, people of color, sex workers, intravenous drug users, immigrants, the homeless. Over time, growing numbers of marginalized people gained a voice as well as influence over AIDS policy, and activist awareness of the toll AIDS was taking globally, especially in African countries, broadened the outcry and added a crucial dimension to the politics of AIDS activism.

It became apparent to survivors in these groups that queer history was being lost to neglect, and to the violent actions of indifferent and hostile biological families who destroyed the effects of their sick and dying relatives. Family shame rationalized the isolation of individuals with AIDS, spurring severance of connection to the lovers, friends, roommates, and partners who had been primary caregivers. The launch of the NAMES Project AIDS Memorial Quilt in 1987 became a prominent cultural response to the relegation of people with HIV to untouchable status, and to the eagerness of the surviving queer community to take collective healing action. Friends, lovers, and supportive family members gathered stories and artifacts to sew into a quilt rectangle that measured roughly the size of a grave plot. The growing collection of panels, each representing the life and memory of one person lost to AIDS, grew to an estimated 1.3 million square feet to become the largest public community artwork in history.

The need to remember individual lives was also behind the emergence of the GLBT Historical Society and its growth from private domestic space to a public archive with professional staff. With the historical tendency for queer history to be erased or forgotten, it became clear that a targeted strategy was called for to preserve queer history—our organizations, our artifacts, our culture and political activism. It was also clear no one else would do this. The infrastructure of activism spawned by AIDS effectively challenged popular social attitudes, government policy, and the medical/pharmaceutical industry. It was in this context that the need to preserve queer history gained urgent and critical traction. In mourning, people were motivated to collect and protect archives more consciously. There are countless stories of community members literally diving into dumpsters to rescue the effects of a person's life from a hostile family's irresponsible disregard.

It was also in this period that a new journal emerged called *OUT/LOOK: National Lesbian and Gay Quarterly*. I was one of six founders, a group of three lesbians and three gay men committed to writing and artwork that reflected diversity in race, gender, genre of writing, and targeted audience—what would later be called intersectionality. My trajectory as both artist and writer started with this collective effort and coincided with my return to college as a late-bloomer art student. I was immersed in a process that connected my role as artist to both activism and intellectual inquiry. Working on *OUT/LOOK* taught me some of the skills that I later brought to my work with the archives at the GLBT Historical Society.

My Lesbian Dilemma

In the early 2000s, I found myself asking, What will I leave behind? What will happen to my artwork, to my old photographs and letters? What about the ephemera I accumulated during four decades of participation in various movements, starting as a white college student marching in support of Black civil rights and protesting the Vietnam War, forming an early consciousness-raising group as part of the women's movement, and embracing the burgeoning gay liberation movement? Buried in boxes in my garage—back then and now—there are archive-worthy materials I should be dealing with: political posters, newspapers, old photographs, vintage typewriters, and three flat files filled with prints. Still fresh in my mind is my mother's fear that her family artifacts would end up tossed in a trash heap.

My concern is a problem of inheritance: What happens to us when we die? Who will remember us? Will anyone even be interested? And no wonder—I come from an extended biological family that was separated by geography before I was born, and an immediate family of seven that was emotionally fractured. My childhood was filled with an acute curiosity about all the secrets rendered mute by my parents: secrets about death and mental illness, suicide, family feuds, buried racial and racist history. My parents were too busy and too uncommunicative to tell stories about their past that might have helped me situate myself. At the start of my work with the GLBT Historical Society, my four siblings and I were the final generation, with no offspring to pass things to or carry our family name. Now, a dozen or so years later, half my family has died, and I inherited the items they left behind. And still there are no other inheritors.

In the late sixties, when I first became aware of the word *lesbian* and shortly afterward met my first homosexuals, I had no framework for understanding same-sex love and desire apart from an acute stabbing fear that felt like a tight grip on my diaphragm. A lurid connection to words like *pervert* and *unnatural* became my most conscious language in the years before Stonewall. When I started to identify as a lesbian at the beginning of the 1970s, I still wondered why and how I fell in love with my first girlfriend. Was this love legitimate? Was I a real lesbian? Not tethered to any awareness of queer history, all I initially had was this turbulent, fearful, and heady new identity, one that came to offer me a closer kind of family than I had ever known. Somewhere in there was my desire for a lineage, for queer roots. I didn't want my life to be yet another family secret, another line on my father's family tree that read "spinster," another buried, invisible existence. I understood viscerally why queer history is important and why it calls for intentional collecting to stave off the oblivion of invisibility. I wanted a connection to a lineage, a history, and a community that would re-imagine family.

Lineage and Community

When I first looked into Larry DeCeasar's archive box, I had just started working with the GLBT Historical Society in an entirely new kind of collaboration. Until then, I had been suffocating in a love/hate relationship to the Art World and an awkward one as an artist in academia. I was ready for something new, something that reached outside both these arenas to engage with people and history in more active ways. My connection to the GLBT Historical Society had existed on and off for years, sometimes as a researcher, other times as a fellow traveler. In 1999, I collaborated with the painter and filmmaker Kim Anno on *Lost & Found, a Museum of Lesbian Memory*, a two-year project sponsored by the organization.

At a 2007 organizational event, board of directors member Don Romesburg casually asked me if I would be interested in joining the board. Although flattered, the thought of more administrative work beyond my academic duties made me shudder. My reply was impulsive, a surprise to both of us: "What I really would like is to be an artist-in-residence." Romesburg, of course, asked what that meant. Once I reassured him it did not mean setting up a cot in the office, he became an enthusiastic sponsor who, armed with a proposal I quickly put together, helped convince the rest of the board that this would be good for the organization. If nothing else, I came free of charge.

What I never revealed was my confusion: Would this be good for me and my art? Would it give me more control over how I put my art out in the world? Would I feel hemmed in, restricted by some form of identity politics that had worn thin by the mid-1990s? There was no room to ask these questions in the cycle of gallery exhibitions and collaborative public art projects I'd been engaged with since getting my master's in fine arts. As an older graduate, I most often felt out of place and invisible in San Francisco's youth-oriented emerging artist scene. Just framing the questions felt like a breath of fresh air, so I decided to go with it. After all, this didn't have to last forever. What excited me was the idea of being embedded in an organization that felt close to my heart, with the possibility of shaking up some of the expectations of what art is and can accomplish. I saw myself as a kind of art catalyst who could perhaps make the archives come alive in unexpected ways.

My prospective work with the GLBT Historical Society had everything to do with an urge to situate my queer life within a community and a history. How could I transform the crisp, detached contents of an archive box into something that might speak and be alive in the present? How could I use art to help expand the reach of the organization? For years, my cross-media approach to art had involved a mishmash of historical research: I studied *Reader's Digest* articles from my childhood; case histories and theories of deviance from across the twentieth century; jump rope rhymes and clapping chants; the unfolding of AIDS in a particular neighborhood; lesbian online dating sites; the history of soap tied to notions of purity and whiteness; lesbian pulp novels from the 1950s; and a variety of gravestone epitaph traditions. I read texts about homosexuality and perversion that ranged from trustworthy to dubious or downright debunked. Sometimes my research was driven by a particular invitation and site; other times it was propelled by a free-ranging curiosity about aspects of the past that have been rendered mute. During each research period, I gradually distilled what I learned into the forms and matter of an artwork. Now, in a relationship to an organization formed to preserve queer history, my research would focus on the contents of the boxes and files in its collections.

Seduction

I was eager to get to work. In an era when fewer security protocols were in place, I was given keys and codes to the locked archive room, a privilege I felt honored, thrilled, and respectful to have earned. It gave my new artist-in-residence title some teeth, the stamp of organizational approval that allowed me to relax into this new identity, this new process of art making and new milieu for research. The first time I walked into the cavernous space of the archive, I remember facing a disorder of boxes on the floor, folders and smaller portfolio boxes on multiple tables, the occasional flag or diva stole poking casually out from a corner. Beyond, a seemingly endless set of tidy aisles disappeared back to a single-point perspective, revealing an oblique view of shelves with their dense arrangements of boxes, lids atop bulging contents, inconsistent labels facing out. I saw familiar names—Harvey Milk, Alan Bérubé, and Del Martin and Phyllis Lyon. Each of these people take up quite a bit of shelf space, with rows and rows for Milk, along with his kitchen table sitting in the back. I photographed that beautiful, distressed table repeatedly, but in the end, these better-known histories did not draw me in. Instead, I found myself attuned to more anonymous voices calling out from certain boxes. An undercurrent of chatter ran through my mind: Who was most interesting? How would I narrow this down? Which collections could help me generate a viable project? During my summer of cruising the aisles, I took copious notes.

My attention turned to the physical presence of a person manifested through their artifacts, sorted by them or someone else and donated to the GLBT Historical Society. As with epitaphs, the contents of the boxes suggested incomplete narratives. I thought, what if I matched a living individual to the archive of someone who had died, fostering a generative relationship? I was drawn to the idea of forging my own relationships to the dead, then opening up each relationship to another person in a kind of three-way connection. Matchmaking in this context held promise as a way to more deeply explore these archives of the dead, to open up their lives to the imagination of living participants.

In this process, DeCeasar's sequined gloves called out to me with palpable urgency; so did objects in other boxes I opened: a love letter written on a red napkin, a framed photo of two women locked in a passionate kiss, an unpublished elaborately annotated sci-fi novel, a certificate of government security clearance, a gold pin in the shape of a penis puncturing a 1940-era body builder postcard, an eight-by-ten-inch photograph of the staff for Dining Hall #3 in Topaz, Utah. These are just a few of the items that captivated me as I walked the aisles of the archive. It was an easy seduction, because I have always found the tangible remains of a person's life uniquely compelling.

It seems I am not alone. I began matching the archives of the dead to living individuals. My open-ended request was that each person create a response to their archive match in the medium of their choice. Each resulting encounter resembled a blind date: I thought about chemistry, demographics, and mutual interests. I created guidelines to later bend: the collections I selected should not be well known, and matches should be between strangers of different generations. I used intuition to pair creative individuals with an unfamiliar archive that might turn them on. The intense dyadic relationships that formed in this process evolved into a form of lineage, one that resides outside of blood-lines and marriage contracts and often outside of identity boundaries. To my surprise, almost everybody I approached responded with enthusiasm. I established protocols for my process of engaging them: make formal introductions between a living participant and their archive, state clearly that there was no obligation to like or commemorate the dead person, and allow the unexpected to unfold in a process of invention that was unique to each participant.

As matchmaker, I found browsing the shelved collections to be somewhat like cruising, threaded with the thrill of chance encounters, the lure of fantasy, the possibility of probing deeper. To open a box, pry apart its folders, touch personal artifacts, scrutinize photos and diary entries is unsettling in its voyeurism. An awareness of death imbues each object with unearthly allure, while what is absent urges further inquiry. Desire was my retrieval mechanism, or maybe it was the fuel: how to select the box, dive in, and open myself to what I discovered inside; how to let myself be fully taken in. There was a distinct feeling of crossing a bound-ary. In the words of one participant, Bill Domonkos, "My experience was unsettling. I felt as if I had stepped into a stranger's house and gone through their drawers."

My process also took place during the period of fervent activism around the legalization of same-sex marriage, in which progress followed a bumpy path. In this fraught con-text, as I prowled the archive aisles, I mused on the question of how to foster intimacy that doesn't fit the marriage model, the kinds of intimacy that dominated my life: close friends, lovers I didn't live with, a fervent independence. And this brought me back around to issues of lineage. Who are my heirs if I am not married and do not have children? And where will my prized belongings go when I'm gone? What will comprise my archive, my legacy to future generations? Accustomed to feeling like an outsider to heterosexual family conventions, suddenly I wondered if I measured up in this new legitimized queer family landscape.

Archives in Motion

The seven-year project I developed eventually got a name: *LINEAGE: Matchmaking in the Archive.* The relationships forged in the matchmaking process generated a powerful body of creative work that over time was exhibited and performed on four continents. It has encompassed live monologue, poetry, an aria sung by a male soprano, several sculptural installations, paintings, photography, personal letters, a jam session, a short film, my dialogical performance collaboration in which I tested notions of lineage— *Affair-on-the-Green*—and my photographic portraits of each matched pair. The sites of exhibition have included galleries, libraries, conferences, an Environmental Protection Agency luncheon, a museum, an archive.

As a kind of ambassador from the arts, the project helped expand people's understanding of what art inspired by archives can be and do. Each public event from the project brought new, diverse people to the GLBT Historical Society, often with standing-room-only audiences. This project became a model for how to engage archives and participants in an open-ended way, a form of social practice in which the invention of a framework for engagement served as the catalyst for new creative works and sometimes new archives.

Matchmaking started at home but, before long, grew complicated by patterns of migration. As the project mushroomed, I started to take the *LINEAGE* project across borders and through customs in a suitcase to create a series of events and exhibitions I called *Migrating Archives.* A presentation at a conference in Brisbane, Australia, in 2010 led to a collaboration and friendship with Karen Charman, a scholar from Melbourne. Her activist approach to academia and interest in biography inspired my first long-distance match—I matched her to a 450-page unpublished memoir by Ruth Reid called *Wife of a Lesbian*, about her twenty-eight-year relationship to Kent Hyde. In a long-distance collaboration, Charman and I wrote about our different psychic and emotional connections to Reid and Hyde (who passed as a man before either second-wave feminism or gay liberation emerged), weaving a textual and visual performance that we carried to a conference at the University of Évora in Portugal. There, in a coincidence that seemed posthumously generous to the archived couple, same-sex marriage had been legalized only the month before.

While visiting ALGA, the Australian Lesbian and Gay Archives (now AQuA, the Australian Queer Archives), in Melbourne, I met a young genderqueer sex worker who became my intern for two months in San Francisco. And I met the director of the organization, Graham Willett. Graham and I connected again at a 2012 queer archive conference in Amsterdam, where I officially launched *Migrating Archives* by enlisting attendees from around the world to select what I called "delegate archives" from their collections. With the help of each organization, I re-presented these archives in an exhibition. Sara De Giovanni, the director of Il Cassero LGBT Center in Bologna, Italy, was one of those who contributed delegate archives. She later invited me to Bologna to be part of their annual Gender Bender festival. The 2015 exhibition *Archivi Migranti: Surrogates from Elsewhere* at Museo d'Arte Moderna di Bologna, showcased delegate archives that were part documentation and part fabricated fiction from Australia, South Africa, Great Britain, the Philippines, Belgium, Hungary, and the United States.

I worked with archivists and directors of twelve archive institutions to identify what could become a metaphorical gift from their organization to Il Cassero, then fabricated interpretations of these gifts in the form of objects, mixed-media arrangements, and sound and animated projections.

Wandering Archives across the Pacific was a project based on connection between artists in two countries and archives that wandered across the Pacific in both directions. For an international art exhibition called *Nothing to Declare*, which was held at several locations in the Philippines during fall 2011, I carried eight creative delegate archives in a suitcase through Manila customs to build an installation called *Mga Sinupang Lagalag (Wandering Archives)* at the Vargas Museum in Quezon City. This work embodied the relationships of eight artists, including me, to the archival artifacts of eight lives. Each of us excavated both tangible traces and gaps in the record to interpret a life. While there, I met Manila archive enthusiasts Giney Villar and Beth Angsioco, owners of Adarna Food and Culture Restaurant, who contributed photographs and correspondence between two gay Filipino men from the early 1900s. This new archive traveled back across the Pacific to become a guest delegate archive at the GLBT History Museum in San Francisco.

Over time, *Migrating Archives* built a lineage between grassroots efforts in Paris, LGBT collections at the British National Archive, a lesbian-owned restaurant and history center in Manila, GALA Queer Archive in Johannesburg, Labrisz in Budapest, ALGA in Melbourne, and many others, including the lonely archive I created as tribute to Ugandan gay martyr David Kato. Archives of the dead were re-invented to travel across borders like delegates from their home archives and cultures. My idea was to put the archives that are precious to each institution into motion as they become guests and hosts, sometimes crossing national borders more easily than we can. As archives migrated across oceans, across national and international borders, I realized I was now fostering relationships between archive organizations. Matchmaking writ large.

Archives are accustomed to sitting on shelves, waiting to be wooed by the occasional researcher. They sit there, fixed in a stasis that is broken only when someone takes them out past the temperature controls, through a locked door, a chance to spread out and receive some attention. The luckiest get to spill their secrets onto written or virtual pages, vicarious wings that connect them to unknown places and people. Archives seldom change; their contents are indexed to larger systems, and so each item must obediently retain its shape and form.

People, on the other hand, wander, sometimes by choice, sometimes by necessity or force. Queer people seem to wander in particular ways. We find each other still through underground routes of site and recognition. Sometimes we migrate to strange cities, looking for signs, sometimes we are free, other times in grave danger. We might nestle into safe zones, with others or alone; we might live publicly, or we might create elaborate masks and risk everything. We have nothing to declare, yet everything. We look for references, we look for a past, and sometimes we invent one.

LINEAGE: Matchmaking in the Archive was an invitation to wander through one archive, to connect with one person for whom selected artifacts have been preserved in boxes and folders. The participants who accepted this invitation became creative agents who were free to interpret a life, to invent a response that ended up being exhibited, performed, read, listened to, or watched by audiences who by and large never knew the archived person. The evolution of the accumulated work transformed many of us in ways we never anticipated. Spending time with the archive of someone who has died is an intense and intimate process; there is an ineffable sadness that occurs. Viewing someone else's artifacts made us think about our own finite lives. Mixed with sadness, there was also an eroticism in touching the artifacts of a life, of entering a narrative that feels private. Would this person have been comfortable with this exploration of their life? Would they be insulted or offended? Was I prying too much? I asked these questions all summer in 2008 as I wandered among the archives of the dead. I wanted to know how participants would navigate these thorny issues, what would come out of the relationships I was fostering. I was eager to discover what would emerge from the recesses of the vault, and I wanted to be surprised.

78

PART 2

Nineteen Conversations
with the Dead

How might a single death be transformed from
an individual occurrence into an occasion for collective praxis?
How can the dead speak through the living as something
other than the haunting, seething presence of absence?
—Molly McGarry, *Ghosts of Futures Past*

The first work to emerge from *LINEAGE: Matchmaking in the Archive* was exhibited at the GLBT Historical Society gallery in fall 2009. I designed the installation to suggest a mirror archive of what lived behind locked doors, and it included the work of the first eleven participants. The piece each person created was displayed on and around steel archive shelving painted white. I fabricated transparent archive boxes to serve as containers and display units for objects from archive collections already matched as well as others waiting in the wings. A line of text, quotations from participants about their relationship to their match person, snaked around the gallery walls. The work of the next eight participants formed the basis for the second *LINEAGE* exhibition, held in 2010 at SOMArts Gallery in San Francisco as an installation within the larger exhibit *Chronotopia*, curated by artist Rudy Lemcke. A smaller selection of work became part of an exhibit at the San Francisco Public Library Main Branch in 2010, organized by Fabled Asp—Fabulous/Activist Bay Area Lesbians with Disabilities: A Storytelling Project.

Each matchmaking story chronicled here begins with a formal portrait of the pair and includes images, text, and descriptions of the response works that the living participants created. While writing this book, more than a decade after they first engaged with the *LINEAGE* project, I asked each participant, "What lingers in your awareness about the project? What would you say to your archive match now?" My camera recorded the chemistry of connection for each matched pair. To create a formal portrait, I posed each living participant in the bright light of a projector image of the dead person so that the living and the dead occupy the frame at the same time. The living participant interacted within the projection to perform their relationship, casting sharp shadows across the picture. Each photo shoot lasted two or three hours; my living subjects frequently spoke to their projected matches, as well as with me and whoever else was in the room. Laughter, discomfort, conversation, and technical distractions all mingled in what felt a bit like a community. In these portrait sessions, the personality of each dyadic relationship came out, exposed in images and sound. Some pairs were shy, slow to warm up. Some participants self-consciously spoke to their ephemeral match through nervous laughter. Others attempted an embrace, speaking intimately, or perhaps teasing. It was during these sessions that I was reminded of nineteenth-century séances and recognized how spirit photographs—tintypes and daguerreotypes in which ghostlike apparitions hovered above the official subject of a portrait—influenced my portraits. The participant Luciano Chessa, who was matched to the archive of Larry DeCeasar, had this to say about his portrait session:

Larry was not my type, yet I was historically intrigued. The only moment in the process in which something took place at a physical level was during the photo session. This is when I actually had to deal with the fact that Larry indeed had a body. As subjects, he and I had to measure our mutual bodies and height, to calibrate the various poses, to make sure I was not covering his face and vice versa—just as with any dual portrait session. Before I knew it, I was flirting with Larry's projection. At times we needed to look each other in the eyes. For some poses Larry was my age and we made a nice couple. In others Larry was an older gentleman with southern sideburns and we played out a daddy aesthetic with me as the younger lover. When Larry sported an Elvis pompadour in one projection, he looked like he'd jumped straight out of a Smiths' album cover. I could not stop thinking of Morrissey!

Tirza True Latimer, an art historian, writer, and faculty emerita at California College of the Arts, helped curate the first *LINEAGE* exhibition. She wrote the following exhibition statement that greeted visitors at the entrance to the GLBT Historical Society gallery.

Historical research on "invisible minorities" engenders unconventional strategies, hones specially adapted skill sets, and relies on resources that may not qualify for conservation in traditional archives. For instance, the seventh sense known as gaydar, a sensitivity to detail that serves queer folks as both a survival mechanism and a social networking device, enables us to recognize and acknowledge kinship outside of nuclear family structures. Personal ephemera and apparently trivial historical detritus—a bodybuilding magazine, a recipe, a page of sheet music, a necktie—can connect us with past lives whose traces would have been lost were it not for archival collections such as those preserved by the GLBT Historical Society. Working with this kind of material calls for the mobilization of techniques frowned on by conventional historians: poetic intervention, speculative re-enactment, storytelling, and fantasy. As Monique Wittig inveighs in *Les Guérillères*, "Remember. Or, failing that, invent." Where there are gaps, we must infer, imagine, project. Or we must take the gap itself as a statement of fact. This exhibition invites such leaps of imagination, projections that illuminate invisible zones within official accounts of historical and biographical events. These archives, animated by creative impulses, unsettle our ideas about who we are, where we come from, who we want to be, and how we remember.

I recently asked Latimer to reflect on the *LINEAGE* project, twelve years later. She writes:

Art historians typically view archives as sources of documentation providing context for the artworks they study. My own art-historical schooling, in the 1990s, conditioned me to view archives as subordinate to artworks. Very few of my mentors and peers recognized archives as wellsprings of creative speculation about histories that remained untold, inaccurate, or incomplete.

The so-called "archival turn," a trend in contemporary artistic practice since the 1960s, has only relatively recently reoriented the practices and publications of scholars. I rounded that corner in 2009, when I accepted E. G. Crichton's invitation to participate in the project *Matchmaking in the Archive*.

Witnessing the queer pasts that E.G.'s archival "matches" illuminated led me to reconsider the status of archival objects, as well as the meta-narrative of the archive itself. Do archives offer evidence of some historical truth, or do they constitute that truth, performatively? Or both? What do unauthorized, shadow, or dissident archives look like and how (differently) do they operate? How might artists, scholars, and activists mobilize even traditional archives more strategically to undermine or reshape belief systems and power structures?

These are only a few of the questions *LINEAGE: Matchmaking in the Archive* continues to raise. In what follows, I tell the story of each matched pair. On facing pages is my formal portrait of the pair, along with images of the living participant's work and items from the archive. The only exception is Barbara McBane and her match Veronica Friedman, whose archive does not include a photograph. Instead of a formal pair portrait, I show excerpts from Barbara's essay and Veronica's archive.

GENTLEMAN'S GAMAN:
A Gay Bachelor's Japanese American
Internment Camp Survival Kit

For: Jiro Onuma
From: Tina Takemoto

The Japanese word "gaman" means enduring the
unbearable with patience & dignity.

Gentleman's Gaman is the art of enduring internment
using found materials, physical culture, and gay
imagination.

THE
EARLE
LIEDERMAN
PHYSICAL
CULTURE
SCHOOL

Tina Takemoto,   Jiro Onuma,
b. 1967   1904–1990

*Gentleman's Gaman (for Jiro Onuma): A Gay Bachelor's Japanese
American Internment Camp Survival Kit*, mixed-media
installation; 2009

When I discovered the amazing collection of Jiro Onuma,
one of the earliest historical records in the GLBT Historical
Society archives, I immediately thought of Tina Takemoto
as a dream match. Takemoto, a queer fourth-generation
Japanese American artist, writer, professor, and academic
dean at the California College of the Arts, was initially skep-
tical. In an essay called "Notes on Internment Camp" in *Art
Journal*, summer 2013, Takemoto wrote:

> I have always been skeptical about matchmaking and
> blind dates. But when the artist E. G. Crichton declared
> that my "perfect match" was a deceased gay Asian Ameri-
> can dandy named Jiro Onuma I was intrigued. . . .
> Crichton set up my first "blind date" with Onuma at the
> Gay, Lesbian, Bisexual, Transgender Historical Society in
> San Francisco, where his personal collection resides.
> Compared to some of the other collections in the archive,
> Onuma's is rather modest, making the details of his life
> quite spare and mysterious. All of his materials fit into a
> slim, six-inch-wide file box containing two photo albums,
> some personal documents and papers, and an assortment
> of homoerotic ephemera.[1]

Onuma was a dandyish—Takemoto's word—gay bachelor who lived in San Francisco for most of his adult life.
He immigrated to the United States from Iwate Prefec-
ture, Japan, in 1923 at age nineteen, arriving in mid-December

after a twenty-day ocean voyage out of Yokohama port. He traveled with his father for this trip and carried among his belongings a beautiful clothbound album with exquisite black-and-white photographs carefully fixed to black pages with embossed photo corners. This album, filled with formal family portraits over two or three generations, includes childhood pictures of Onuma with his sister. Family members are dressed in traditional Japanese attire in some photos, in Western attire in others. I could find no clues about his reasons for immigrating to the United States but can speculate that being gay might have made him restless. This was also the same year that the Great Kanto Earthquake devastated Tokyo and Yokohama on September 1, 1923, disrupting life in the entire region.

Before World War II, Onuma worked at Mercury Laundry and Cleaners in the area now known as the Tenderloin district of San Francisco. His archive includes photographs of him posed with Japanese American friends during the 1920s and 1930s. The archival materials also show that Onuma collected male fitness magazines and was a fan of the pioneer bodybuilder and trainer Earle E. Liederman, well known to gay men of that era. Onuma's box includes a brochure titled *Art Folio of Muscular Marvels*, a postcard of a man in a matador costume with a small gold penis pin piercing the card stock, and a medal of achievement from the Earle Liederman Physical Culture School. Other items in his collection include passports, driver's licenses, small photograph albums, a mounted formal photograph of Onuma in a black dress suit, tourist pictures and maps, a small telephone book, health insurance cards, bank statements, and his selective service notice of classification 4-C (alien or dual national), dated October 20, 1942.

Onuma's life was severely disrupted by Executive Order 9066, which the U.S. government issued on February 19, 1942. Along with 120,000 other Japanese Americans, he was forcibly removed, first to the Tanforan temporary detention facility just south of San Francisco. Seven months later, he was incarcerated in the Topaz concentration camp in Topaz, Utah, at the age of thirty-eight. It was Takemoto who observed that two photos in Onuma's archive were taken inside a camp, one showing the guard tower in the background, another a formally posed group of workers in the Block #3 mess hall taken in July 1943. In this photo, Onuma, small and slight, is seated cross-legged in the front row, right. Another photograph shows Onuma with a man named Ronald, whose family name is unknown, but whose portrait appears multiple times in Onuma's private albums. Takemoto speculates that Ronald and Onuma were in a relationship and that Ronald sent one of the photographs of himself and his friends to Onuma from the Tule Lake concentration camp in California. After two years, Onuma was released from Topaz on May 16, 1944, and went first to Salt Lake City to work and later to Denver for two years.

Onuma returned to San Francisco, where he held jobs as a presser at the Pine Street Laundry and later as a janitor at a residential hotel on Eddy Street, where he also lived. In 1956, Onuma attained naturalized citizen status. Language embedded in the certificate of naturalization exposes the racism of the period: his complexion is entered on the form as "sallow." Passports in his archive indicate that he returned to Japan several times in the 1980s to visit his family. His passports are stamped with other travel destinations as well, including Machu Picchu, Peru; Thailand; and various European countries. Takemoto discovered that he eventually worked as a butler for a Caucasian doctor in San Francisco. When he died at age eighty-six on June 27, 1990, he was living alone in his apartment at 1550 O'Farrell Street. His archive includes three copies of the death certificate, which indicates chronic obstructive pulmonary disease and hypertensive heart disease as cause of death. He was buried in the Japanese cemetery in Colma, California.

Once I introduced the two, Takemoto pored over Onuma's archive and embarked on extensive research outside the framework of the collection. They enlisted their partner's mother to help translate kanji characters on the backs of photographs in the archive. Takemoto also studied narratives and records about life in Japanese American incarceration camps, about the arts and crafts prisoners were able to create, and about their work lives. In acts of performative empathy, Takemoto learned how to whittle wood and how to make use of materials that were available in the camp, such as tar paper and pine scraps. At one point they reported to me on injuries they sustained in this process: small cuts from the whittling knife, burns from bringing out invisible lemon juice drawings with a flame, muscle strain from testing an invented exerciser strap. Throughout, Takemoto used a kind of imaginative ingenuity to conjure Onuma's life as a lonely gay man among his fellow Japanese inmates.

The project Takemoto created for the first *LINEAGE* exhibition was an installation that included handcrafted objects Onuma might have needed or wanted: a wallet and a cigarette holder made from tar paper, carved bird cufflinks and a tie clip, a *gaman*-style Hanafuda card set on tar paper cards with muscle men figures instead of the traditional flowers, a homemade progressive exerciser device with a chart to record progress, and a gold medal made from flour, compliments of the Earle Liederman Physical Culture School. The objects were displayed on a set of white steel archive shelves.

In Takemoto's words:

> I grew up hearing family stories about the prison camps, but no one ever mentioned the gay and lesbian experience of imprisonment. I try to imagine how Jiro Onuma survived the isolation, boredom, humiliation, and heteronormativity of incarceration in Topaz, Utah, as a dandyish gay bachelor from San Francisco who was obsessed with erotic male physical culture magazines. From Onuma's archive, I discovered that he enrolled in Earle Liederman's 12-week correspondence Physical Culture School program. Was he receiving letters from Liederman and following this program in camp as a way to keep his queer imaginary alive? Jiro Onuma is my gay Japanese American role model, queer accomplice, and friend.

After the exhibition, Takemoto continued to pursue a relationship to Onuma through other projects. They published an article titled "Looking for Jiro Onuma: A Queer Meditation on the Incarceration of Japanese Americans during World War II."[2] They created an animated film based on the process of holding a flame under a soy sauce drawing of three friends of Onuma, showing a guard tower looming in the background. The drawing gradually disappears into cinders. In their most ambitious work, Takemoto created a compelling music video drag performance in which they reenacted Onuma working in the Topaz mess hall, kneading and braiding strands of dough to fit around their arms as simulated imaginary muscles. The music of the ABBA song

"Gimme! Gimme! Gimme! (A Man after Midnight)" along with Madonna's song "Hung Up," with its repeated refrain "Time goes by so slowly," plays throughout, and historical war propaganda footage from various Japanese American incarceration camps is interspersed and manipulated to form a hilarious and poignant representation of repetitious routines in the camp.

Throughout their process, Takemoto continued to ask the question, "Is it possible to form personal and affective attachments to queer individuals and absent memories through the objects and materials they have left behind? . . . This mode of working through the archive reflects not only my own longing for a connection to Onuma's material but also my grief over the impossibility of fully reanimating his partial and fragmented traces of remembrance."

In crafting their interpretation of Onuma's life, Takemoto's work has made Onuma feel familiar, knowable across the decades, both sympathetic and admirable. His archive offers an amazing view into a gay immigrant's working-class life in the early twentieth century and, later, of the horrific mid-century wartime removal and incarceration of Japanese Americans. Takemoto imagined Onuma's additional isolation as a gay man. His life was both ordinary and extraordinary, and Takemoto's way of forming a relationship with him brings this into poignant focus.

Twelve years after I first matched Takemoto to Onuma, the artist expressed these thoughts:

My encounter with Jiro Onuma through E. G. Crichton's *Matchmaking* project transformed my art practice as well as my relationship to Japanese American wartime history. Onuma's archive put me directly in touch with the lesser-known history of same-gender-loving Japanese immigrants. The photographs and artifacts that he left behind offer some provocative clues about the life he lived. But so much of his story belongs to the realm of speculation. His life and legacy have inspired me to expand my artistic investigation of queer Asian American ancestors. If I was able to speak to Jiro Onuma today, I would ask him to share some of the highlights of living in gay San Francisco in the 1930s.

Bill Domonkos,   Helen Harder,
b. 1960   1918–1984

The Poppy, experimental film; 2009

Discovering the Helen Harder box in the archives ignited my
own romantic fantasies as much as any twenty-first-century
figure might. There she was in her World War II Army Air
Force jacket, standing next to a Piper Cub aircraft, helmet
in hand and parachute ready in her backpack. Damn, she was
handsome. Not always attracted to a woman in uniform,
I found that this one—safely ensconced in the past—got
to me. All that pent-up sexual power held in check by will,
with just the right touch of vulnerability, reached out to me
from the exquisite black-and-white silver gelatin print.

Maybe that is why I matched Harder with a gay man, the
filmmaker Bill Domonkos. Domonkos, who relocated from
Oakland, California, to Detroit in 2017, creates experimental
films scored with original soundtracks. He is the ultimate film
buff. In another coincidence that bolstered my confidence as a
matchmaker, when I introduced Domonkos to Harder's
archive, he told me that his favorite film of all time, *Wings*, is
about a Russian woman who was also a World War II pilot.
Both women, on opposite sides of the Cold War, became single mothers, and both had a difficult time adjusting to life after
the war. For his contribution to the project, Domonkos created
a short experimental film called *The Poppy*, inspired by one of
Harder's poems. Using a combination of manipulated archive
film footage, digital animation, and special effects, Domonkos's
film evokes an inner landscape of poetic juxtapositions about
identity, isolation, longing, and alienation. He wrote:

    I was immediately attracted to the deeply personal poetry
    Helen had written with titles like "Melancholia," "The

Poppy," "Mediation of a Lonely Heart," "Soliloquy of Despair," "Invocation to Death," and "Madness." As someone attracted to the darker side of human nature, I was captivated by Helen's personal, uncompromised poetic voice. I created *The Poppy* using a series of film loops that change and evolve over time. The woman in the film is stuck in a loop of conflict between her inner and outer nature. It's funny, the woman in the film kind of resembles a woman Helen had a crush on from pictures in her archive.

Some of Harder's poetry can be found in her archive box, including "The Poppy." Typed on delicate onionskin paper with a cigarette burn mark over its title, it reads:

A languor has come over me; I live
    As if in dreams. The muffled roar
Of turquoise sea on golden strand can give
    Me now but sadness; nothing more.
The yellow poppy is within my veins;
    My one desire is repose.
The sluggish blood no greater power retains
    Than breathing perfume of a rose.
O, Soul, arise! Shake off these pleasant dreams.
    Hie thee away where duty calls.
Much yet undone—but those are hopeless schemes;
    I am a pris'ner in these walls.

I wonder, is this about desire or drugs? Or is it just utter despair? Other verses are equally dark, with references reminiscent of Emily Dickinson: "Something died in me last night—it was my heart," "Strange love that never lets me go . . ." and "The barriers of anguish, pride and bitter words / Are stronger far than man-made buttresses."

The black-and-white photographs in her box show group-ings of women in uniform, warm expressions indicating they were most likely friends, and I wonder which one of these women broke Harder's heart. In another photo, from 1945, two couples in civilian clothes are seated in the club Finoc-chio's in San Francisco, which was famous for its drag shows. The foursome sits squeezed close together on one side of a table, a man on either end, the two women in the middle. Harder scratched their names in ballpoint pen across the top border: "Bobby, me, Toby, Ken." At first it appears to be a heterosexual double date, but a closer inspection reveals a view underneath the table of Toby's hand resting on Harder's knee in an unmistakably intimate and sexy gesture. Was Toby her long-lost love? Harder kept the Finocchio's program from that evening in 1945 for forty years. Like the other materials in her box, this photograph was donated to the GLBT Histori-cal Society by her son, Arion Stone, after she died.

The archive of Harder, born Eleanor F. Sugg in 1918 in North Carolina, includes a single pink hand-knitted baby bootee and a high school photograph of her standing under a tree holding a German shepherd puppy and sporting an extremely short boys' haircut that would hardly have been in fashion in the mid-1930s. She is dressed in loose white pants and a white shirt with the sleeves rolled up. At the bottom of the label, "Me" is written in ballpoint pen.

Much of what I found in her box pertained to her service in World War II: a worn leather folder honorable discharge from the U.S. Army; photographs of friends in uniform, mostly women; several pins with military insignia. She was a flight instructor in the Women's Army Corps (WAC) and received an honorable discharge in 1944. Some of what we know of her is from an oral interview conducted by the late Alan Bérubé, historian, activist, independent scholar, and co-founder of the San Francisco Lesbian and Gay History Project. His research and interviews related to World War II resulted in the publication of *Coming Out under Fire* in 1990, the first definitive history of the hidden freedoms some enlisted lesbians and gays experienced during the Second World War.[3]

After the war, Harder worked in factories and canneries before earning her teaching credentials to become an elementary school teacher. She was interested in spirituality, and her archive includes several essays she wrote on the subject. There are also astrology charts and a photo of abstract white lights against a mottled yellow-and-orange background, an aura reading, according to a label on the back. Among her ephemera is a pin that reads "ERA Campaign 1972–1982." In the early 1980s, she helped organize a National Organization of Women (NOW) chapter in rural Nevada; her archive includes the financial records for the organization. A *San Francisco Examiner* news clipping she saved from June 29, 1981, has the headline "200,000 Homosexuals Parade."

Harder raised her son, Arion Stone, as a single mother. The year before my first encounter with Harder's archive, this son brought a new item to donate to the GLBT Historical Society: Harder's 1940s-era light gray vibrator in its own custom box with multiple attachments. The plastic is somewhat cracked, the cord a little frayed, but it otherwise seems to be in working order. I displayed it in a transparent archive box as part of the first *LINEAGE* exhibition, the one where Domonkos's film *The Poppy* was shown. News that Stone was coming to the reception for this show made me nervous. I wondered how he would feel about the way I was using his mother's life in this matchmaking process. So far, dealing with the archives of the dead had not brought issues of accountability to them into my project. But Stone was friendly, and I later found out that he approved. I feel much less certain that Harder would have approved, at least in regard to having her vibrator on public display.

I have questions I wish I could ask Harder: about her unhappy poetry, her astrological charts, her aura photograph, her writings on spirituality. And about her baby, the son she apparently raised as a single mother, named after an ancient Greek poet. Nowhere in the archive could I find clues about a father, a husband, or a woman lover with whom she shared parenting. Did Harder find a way to inseminate? Did she have a one-night affair, maybe with a gay man? Was the father's name Stone? Someday I will find Arion Stone and ask him.

I asked Domonkos recently for his thoughts about Harder and the work he created over a decade ago. He writes:

> Back then, I felt like I broke into someone's house and was going through their personal things. I still feel that way. I don't know that she would have wanted anyone to see those personal things; I certainly would not. So that has made me even sadder to think she had no control over this. The things in her archive were very personal and my response was to the overwhelming loneliness that came through her letters, poems, documents, and images. One thing that still haunts me is the Polaroid of a single flower in a vase on her coffee table, which sparked my film *The Poppy*. The thing is, I wonder if I would have had this same impression of her had I known her in the flesh. Thinking of the stuff I might leave behind, I'm not so sure that would give much insight into who I really am as a person. So, I guess I'm left with the impression that once we're gone we really don't have any control over our legacy. I hope what remains of me does not end up in an archive somewhere. I prefer to just vanish, without a trace. Working with Helen's archive certainly made me aware of the LGBT struggles of her time. Her loneliness and her search for meaning still haunt me.

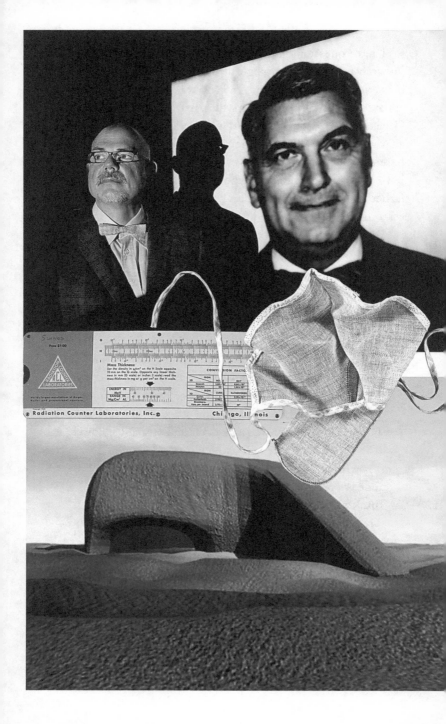

Elliot Anderson,
b. 1960

Claude *René* Schwob,
1910–2000

> *unsanitized*, 3-D video animation with public
> domain footage and original animation; 2009

The match between the media artist Elliot Anderson and the scientist Claude René Schwob started with an affinity for slide rules. Among other things, Anderson is a collector, and his home is filled with pristine assortments of dishes, chairs, handmade toolboxes, and lava lamps. He describes himself as a hoarder with good taste. I remember slide rules from grade school math and science and, at one time, knew how to use one. They were an item we had to buy for school, along with pencils and erasers. For Anderson, this is a vintage item—by the time he needed to calculate, electronic pocket calculators were in common use. I didn't realize until I introduced him to the Schwob archive that Anderson had stashed away a collection of slide rules. One box holds two elegant examples of this archaic computing tool still encased in their original sleeves. Anderson was practically drooling, and I realized this was a perfect match.

The archives of Schwob, Jiro Onuma, and Helen Harder present three contrasting lives lived in relation to the Second World War. Schwob was a government chemist involved in the development of the atomic bomb. His papers document his professional, personal, and erotic life. Born in New York, he grew up in France and received his advanced degrees in chemistry from Fordham University in New York City in 1931. A decade later, he enlisted in the U.S. Army, volunteering for the Chemical Warfare Service. This led to his work on the Manhattan Project, the government research and development effort that invented the first nuclear weapons. After the war, Schwob moved from Los Alamos, New

Mexico, to San Francisco to work at the U.S. Naval Radiological Defense Laboratory in Bayview-Hunters Point, becoming one of the nation's foremost experts on radiation. The focus of his work was identifying safe ways of detecting, preventing, and responding to radiation exposure.

According to Schwob's obituary in the *Bay Area Reporter* on September 14, 2000: "Schwob loved San Gregorio beach, the Russian River, the pool at the Oasis, beautiful men, and photography. He supported programs for homeless gay youth, such as Hospitality House. During much of his adult life, Schwob collected or took photographs of nude men, and accumulated a large number of these prints. The donor of his papers, Trent R. Dunphy, claims that Schwob continued to be sexually active until close to his death at age ninety."

There were apparently enough erotic photographs in Schwob's archive to warrant the archive's warning label: "The erotica in this collection may only be viewed by researchers age eighteen and over, and it is made available for educational and research purposes only." These photographic prints were unusual in that they depicted male nudes without erections. Though Anderson thinks he remembers photos of Schwob re-enacting a fanciful comradery from his army days in more overtly sexual poses, he readily acknowledges, "Maybe I just made this up." I don't remember the photographs much, but I do clearly remember meticulously preserved papers and artifacts, including the two slide rules. I remember matchbooks from bars set in neat grids in two plastic sleeves and other documents ranging from personal correspondence to public notices, all carefully sleeved. Though Schwob's collection is still unprocessed by an archivist, careful curating clearly went in to preserving it. By whom, I wonder? Did Schwob, with an eye to preserving his legacy, put this archive together, or did the donor of the materials do it posthumously with an eye to history?

As I revisited my photo documentation of Schwob's archive, I remembered other artifacts. There are images of two issues of the *Santa Fe New Mexican* following the drop of the first bomb on Hiroshima; a diploma from Saint Ann's Academy in New York City; a huge cartoon-drawn map of the activities of the Twenty-Ninth Infantry Division; a certificate with a cum laude gold seal from Fordham University; a trophy inscribed with the label "U.S. Naval Radiological Defense Laboratory / San Francisco, Calif / Claude R. Schwob / March 15, 1948–April 20, 1964"; a membership card with "Leather Fraternity member in good standing / Drummer Key Club / exp. 6-82"; and a note reading "Sweetheart / Thank you for Everything / Will see you soon. / P.S. call me 673-1849 / Love ya Terry B. XXXX."

A carefully typed poem or diary entry (it is impossible to tell), dated Tuesday, February 15, signed "TW," contains the lines "Why do we have war? / Why are we suffering? / . . . He became for me more than a friend, more than a brother, more than my love / More . . . much more . . . !!." The text continues on February 18 with lines alluding to a vision of one man dying to save another on the battlefield. Anderson speculates that this antiwar poem, seeped in homoerotic visions of martyrdom, would have been a security risk in the highly sensitive arena where Schwob worked. Other documents surely would have been: a sleeved combination of newspaper clippings, one a torn map of Griffith Park in Los Angeles, with a caption that reads "Combat Zone." The map shows the area where police rounded up gay men in an operation called Fire Hazard. Next to this clipping is a neatly cut-out undated article from the *San Francisco Chronicle* column Question Man by Keith Power, in which "How would you commit suicide?" is asked at Fifth and Jessie Street. And in another sleeve is a folded issue of the *San Francisco Free Press* from 1969 with the huge headline

"Homosexual Civil War." In a separate sleeve, a typed directory page has the header "Drug, Counseling, Psychiatric Problems," below which various psychiatric services are listed: suicide hotlines, help centers for LSD; at the bottom, under "Homosexual Associations," are entries for Council on Religion and the Homosexual, Daughters of Bilitis, and Society for Individual Rights (SIR). This range of clippings, which span gay martyrdom, police violence, and efforts at resistance, reveals subjects that clearly preoccupied Schwob during his life.

Buried deeper in the archive, I found a letter addressed to Schwob at Fordham University that used the coded language of the closet:

My dear Claude:

I wish to thank you for your letter of May 31st, relative to the matter which we have already discussed.

Let me assure you that there is no need for any worry in this matter, since I have investigated and have discussed the matter in a very impersonal way. Hence, you must not feel that there is any necessity for rehabilitation of yourself in my estimation.

I am confident, dear Claude, that everything will succeed in your case, and for this I pray and hope most earnestly.

With very kind personal greetings to you, I am
Very sincerely yours,

Aloysius J. Hogan, S.J.

A quick internet search revealed that Hogan was a Jesuit priest and president of Fordham University during the period when Schwob both attended and taught classes. I wonder, was Schwob caught with another man?

Anderson became intrigued by Schwob's ability to navigate his role as a gay scientist while working on the high-security Manhattan Project and, later, his production of the photographs of nude men. Anderson refers to Schwob as a transitional character who appeared to be comfortable with his sexuality at a time in history when the risks were high for gay men. In his response to Schwob's archive, he asked: "How do we penetrate open secrets? This is the question that stands out for me when I think about Claude and his work. He never married, he had relationships with men, he shot erotic photos and yet worked in the most secretive of military research at a time when the federal government was purging LGBTQ employees in fear they would be subjected to blackmail and divulge government and military secrets to the Soviets."

Growing up at the end of the "duck and cover" generation, a phrase that refers to protective actions that were officially recommended during the Cold War, Anderson has his own early memories of bomb drills and fallout shelters. For this project, he pored over recently declassified films of atomic bomb tests in the Pacific Ocean, selecting excerpts to blend with his own animation. The resulting video uses a repeated image of an underground shelter to frame a narrative about subconscious desires and destruction. Using the redacted contents of the military language in the government films, Anderson crafted an original sound composition that spliced together ghostly voices as they recount the destruction in clinical tones and language. The title of Anderson's video, *unsanitized*, is an ironic double negative alluding to redacted secrets that are both revealed and simultaneously concealed. "Sanitizing" is how the military frames the release of redacted classified information. The prologue to the found films states that the material had been sanitized for wider military distribution and viewing, implying that there is still something we don't know and aren't supposed to know. The materials in Schwob's archive reflect an important history that is still being sanitized and redacted.

Along with the image of the shelter, Anderson's video features the solitary figure of an engineer with his slide rule, a guide to a devastated world. Underground, the world is destroyed, and houses and neighborhoods are wiped out in radioactive storms. His piece ends with a view of the shirt-less bodies of the soldiers exposed to radiation as they survey the debris. Their fears and the damage to the cells of their bodies are secrets. Anderson wrote:

> Claude helped engineer the future. He was a gay in the military industrial complex with an eye for the boys. He was the bomb. ~~unsanitized~~ is a media work that reveals as much as it hides. A straight co-worker of mine once stood up in a manager's meeting and said, "So what if he's gay, he's a good employee and a good gay." That's when I became officially a good gay. Engineers are most often fearful of their sexuality. How did Claude survive the most secretive of military programs with his sexuality intact? But it seems to be the case. Photos of him in uniform with loves and sex partners, those boudoir shots of young men, and proud credentials of his participation in Operation Apache—an A-bomb test at Bikini Atoll— all live in one box. He was a good (and not so good) gay.

I recently asked Anderson to think back to his work with Schwob's archive ten years ago. He writes:

> In hindsight his personal celebration of his military work left me uneasy. I remember how some of the Schwob documents contain circled notes of pride: "I did this!" Schwob was part of the "Greatest Generation" that

returned triumphant after WWII. I was born in 1960, which was the beginning of the dramatic upheaval and change that formed a violent chasm between generations. Growing up near an army base I saw first-hand what war does to those who fight it. The church we attended was on the army base and there were pews removed for men who were disabled in Vietnam. I still carry those images with me.

I can't imagine how Schwob maintained an active and at least partly open gay life. His experience resonates with my own in some ways. I studied computer engineering as an undergraduate and worked as an engineer in the 1980's. My last engineer job fired me because of my HIV diagnosis—and for being gay.

Schwob's archive has given me a new framework for understanding the lives of LGBTQ people from the past. Working with his material inspired me to shift my research and artmaking to find lives like his and share them with a larger audience. I am currently developing a project to tell the story of the South of Market Neighborhood and the LGBTQ/Leather community that lived and played there. In 2017 the City of San Francisco and LGBTQ/Leather community organizations, businesses and individuals unveiled a monument to the history of individuals and organizations that gave birth to and sustained the South of Market community. I'm developing a documentary about this history that will be told through an app for the site. Schwob will be there with me as I dive into the archives again.

Lauren Crux,
b. 1947

Janny MacHarg,
1923–2003

Dinosaurs and Haircuts, live solo performance
and artist's book; 2009

The archive collection of Janny MacHarg is one I discovered
early on; the flamboyance of its contents called out to me like
a beacon, pointing me to the person represented inside. In
one standard archive box, forty-eight carefully labeled manila
folders were packed tightly along with a white vinyl three-
ring binder. In a large flat box, two items of clothing were
folded neatly, as though just purchased from a department
store. The archive donation form indicated three donor
names, including a therapist I once saw with a lover as we
crashed and burned through our breakup.

Who was this MacHarg who crossed paths with my life
so obliquely? The penciled labels on the folders indicate
subjects such as "Correspondence," "Written by Others,"
"Interview," "Death Notices," "Drawings," "Flyers," "GLOE
[Gay and Lesbian Outreach to Elders]," "Conference of Old
Lesbians," "Writings A–Z." The clothing box contained a
green satin robe, a long black dress with feathers on the cuffs,
and a gold-colored brooch. I photographed these items repeatedly and sketched them in my notebook. Inserted into the
cover of the binder was a copy of a photo showing a woman
dressed in the black dress—it must be MacHarg—sitting at a
piano, playing and looking out at the photographer, the audience, looking at me. Inside this binder, I found song lyrics
and other writings, a scrapbook, notices of performances, and
more photographs. Her original songs revealed her progressive
politics and elder activism: "Janny Sings for Love and Freedom" and "Aging Is Not for Sissies." A song from her teenage
years, copyrighted 1940, was titled "Naughty Green Eyes."

There were six audiocassette tapes in a plastic baggie that had seen better days.

In the midst of my excavation, I decided that my friend Lauren Crux would be the perfect match for this flamboyant, political songwriter and cabaret performer. The previous year, I had collaborated with Crux to choreograph a performance conversation titled *Affair-on-the-Green*, which addressed notions of lineage. Crux is also a performer with her own kind of flamboyance, a writer who develops monologues with titles like *My Lunch with Sophia Loren*, *The Study of Nouns*, *On Being Cool, and Other Digressions*, and *Beige Dreams*. As an interdisciplinary artist, Crux works with photography, video, movement, poetry, and sculptural props. In one way or another, she is always asking, "How does one enter into an intimacy with all things?" Crux is also a psychotherapist by trade and recognized the names of many of the therapists who attended MacHarg's memorial service. These elements led me to believe Crux and MacHarg were made for each other.

Crux was not so sure, but she dove in, photographing the clothing and folders, reading through correspondence and song lyrics, looking at all the fading xeroxed photographs and promotional flyers. Crux learned that MacHarg had been nicknamed "the Tallulah Bankhead of San Francisco," after the famous stage actress of the mid-twentieth century who came from a prominent Alabama conservative political family. Bankhead became notorious for her support of civil rights and her opposition to the dictator Francisco Franco in the Spanish Civil War, as well as her promiscuous bisexuality and her alcoholism and drug addiction, all of which she spoke about publicly. Crux came to me early on with doubts: "I'm not sure I like Janny; I'm not sure I would have even been friends with her." I reassured Crux that "liking an archive match" was not a requirement of the project.

Not until Crux located a tape player and played Mac-Harg's six cassette tapes did something start to shift. She wrote:

> Think about being on a blind date: the awkwardness, the hopefulness, the disappointments, the not-knowing. That's what it was like to begin this process. I kept wanting to bail on the whole thing. But then something happened, and I came to not only appreciate but to have warm fuzzy feelings for Janny. She loved a good story well-told, and she knew the power of humor to bypass the brain and go straight to the heart. I think Janny and I would have liked each other, even though I don't smoke, have never liked martinis, and prefer a white tux to a black evening gown. She has gone straight to my heart.
>
> At first I related to Janny as my butch buddy—until her friend Ida B. Red clued me in that she was femme and described her favorite red leather jacket, fuel for my subsequent fantasy. When I finally heard her songs on tape, I fell in love. She had a deep bawdy humor, and I wanted to know her. I am creating a friendship with a dead person. I notice the shift to present tense. I find myself writing, Janny will like this story. . . . Now I have to remind myself I never actually met her.

Through her process of getting to know MacHarg archivally, Crux developed a performance monologue called *Dinosaurs and Haircuts*, which she performed on the opening night of the first *LINEAGE* exhibition. This piece was about a blind date, about old lesbians and intimations of mortality, about what we leave behind. For an object to display in the physical exhibition, she created an oversize coffee-table artist's book with the same title, filled with images and text that recorded the ephemeral performance in tangible graphic beauty. Part of Crux's monologue went like this:

> An editor of a feminist journal posed the question: Are lesbians becoming extinct? Hmmm. Sometimes I feel like a dinosaur among haircuts, and from time to time I do ask myself some questions: Am I still a lesbian? Is our post-modern understanding of the fluidity of gender and sexuality and identity making my identity irrelevant? Is the word "Queer" truly inclusive, or does it serve to erase me? Or am I already erased? Am I soon to be a relic—Oh look, an old lesbian, how quaint? I am so fond of lesbians; I like to hold them in my arms, to touch them, feel them. . . . It seems as though it took me so long to get here. Back when I came out, we didn't exist then either. We have not had a long run. I'd like to linger just a bit longer.

MacHarg herself was profoundly visible as a life-long activist and lesbian. In a report by the California Senate Interim Committee in 1949 on un-American activities, MacHarg is listed as involved with a "Trojan horse camouflage" at the California Labor School at the University of California, Berkeley, as both teacher and participant. The point seemed to be that communists had infiltrated the university curriculum. Both MacHarg and Evie Turner, her Black partner of fifty-four years, were thrown out of the Communist Party for being lesbians. At MacHarg's memorial in 2003, a member of the Communist Party named John, the son of one of MacHarg's former comrades in the party, stood up to speak a belated formal apology, crediting his father with initiating the gesture. This was one of many memories shared by people who attended the opening night reception for the *LINEAGE* exhibit, people who had known MacHarg in life. She was involved with a number of familiar organizations: Mothertongue Feminist Theater Collective, Options for Women Over 40 theater group, Gray Panthers, Older Women's League, Women's Alcoholism Center, Freedom Song Network, New Leaf, and Older Lesbians Organizing for Change (OLOC). A promotional flyer lists MacHarg among the planning committee members for West Coast Celebration II and the 1989 Conference of Old Lesbians.

At the time of her work with MacHarg's archive, Crux asked the question: "When I'm dead, will there be a younger lesbian who takes an interest in me?" Recently reflecting on her archival relationship to MacHarg, Crux writes:

> Janny does not linger with me in the sense of loitering. She was not the loitering type, so she never got stuck in there. But I think of her as a friend from long-ago. We knew each other well-enough and liked and appreciated each other—I have a weakness for irreverence and wit, and I admire courage. When I think of her, I always say "hello" and smile and give her an imaginary hug. I see that I am writing as if we actually knew each other in contemporary embodied time.
>
> And I did, through this project, come to know her in certain ways—her music, her poetry, her dress, her gloves. Her alcoholism; her depression; her recovery; her fears. Her laughter. Her love of performing. It was a big relief when two of her friends told me after my performance that I had "got her right." I wanted to honor her that way. I still remember the visceral feeling of opening Janny's archive box. The sense of slightly creepy fear, a wanting to turn away. But then allowing myself to enter in, to get to know someone. Whenever I enter into something new, I enter slowly, cautiously, then jump in. It was that way with Janny.
>
> The other day, I was thinking of her because there is a new friend I wanted to introduce her to. Someone

extroverted, irreverent, with a taste for the provocative, opinionated and bossy, and also, as Janny would say, "OLD"—she's 92. I thought to myself, "Oh they will like each other." Again, in present tense. So yes, Janny lives on in me. As with my new friend, I don't think I would have been close to Janny. Too much smoke, too much guarded-ness and prickliness. But friends, yes. For sure. And respect.

When I think of friends who are younger than me and who, if all goes well, will outlive me, I wonder how they will hold me in memory. I wonder what objects of mine, if any, they will keep or treasure. What will get tossed away as junk? In Janny's archive box there is an emerald green dress. I have also saved an emerald green velvet full-length sleeveless dress my sister made for me when I was 20. Even after I came out I wore this dress to big events, because it looked good and I liked wearing something sexy, elegant and formal to complicate my butchiness.

I hope that Janny somehow knows that she made a difference in people's lives, in my life. She affected me and I carry her with me.

Crux recently reminded me about our photo portrait shoot eleven years ago. One night in my campus studio, I projected several images of MacHarg on a wall, then posed Crux inside of the cast light. For this occasion, Crux wore a white tuxedo. She loved that the image I eventually selected was one in which MacHarg was also decked out in formal attire in her long black evening dress, the one now preserved in an archive box. Crux's memory of the two hours we spent trying out different poses was that we laughed a lot as I worked my camera and Crux gazed at MacHarg, sometimes speaking to her, other times addressing me. The three of us had a great time. Looking back now, Crux realizes she had never really thought about lineage before and never been the slightest bit interested in archives. But that shifted as she became excited by the process of connecting to MacHarg at the different stages of her life, of writing a performance that spoke to and about MacHarg as she got to know her. Linear time seemed to evaporate as Crux navigated this connection and thought about her own life's trajectory.

I recently dragged a stool over to look at my collection of old journals on the top shelf of my living room bookcase. There I found an old *Sinister Wisdom* issue with the theme "Old Lesbians/Dykes." It included a short personal essay by MacHarg called "Niche Picking."[4] With what I've come to recognize as her characteristic sly humor, MacHarg describes tensions within her family about who will occupy cremation urns in the niche of her mother, Gaga, at Chapel of the Chimes in Oakland, California. The problem is that there are more future dead people than spaces available and paid for. MacHarg's niece Sherry insists that her own mother's urn cannot sit next to that of MacHarg's bigoted sister Chloe and brother-in-law Morty for all eternity. Sherry wants MacHarg and her longtime partner, Evie Turner, to fill the remaining spaces in order to block Chloe and Morty. But, MacHarg writes, "Evie insists on her ashes being scattered, and if she wants that, I want it too." She continues, "It has all worked out to perfection so far, thanks to our Higher Power. . . . My mother and Claire (beloved older sister) are side by side in the Court of the Everlasting on top of the hill at eye level." In an addendum labeled "Cryptic Note," Mac-Harg finishes: "My niece Sherry told me that her friend Yvette was scattering her husband's ashes when a small piece of him flew back and lodged in her eye. She had to be rushed to the emergency hospital. When I tell Evie, maybe she will change her mind—there is still room for two in Gaga's niche."

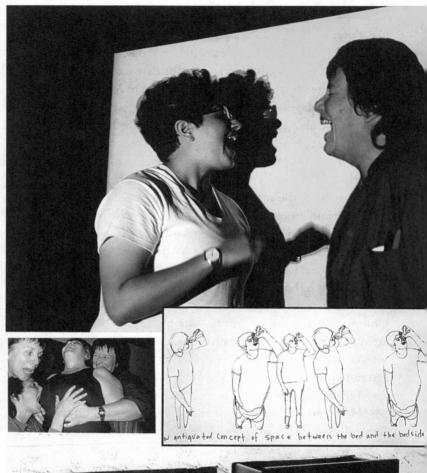

w antiquated concept of space between the bed and the bedside

Maya Manvi,					Dodi Horvat,
b. 1987						1940–1989

Tools for (Re)Construction/Ruelle,
mixed-media installation; 2009

Berkeley, California, resident Maya Manvi, who is a video
and sculpture artist as well as an art teacher at Mission High
School in San Francisco, was the youngest person seated at
the table for *Affair-on-the-Green*, the 2008 performance
conversation that I orchestrated with Lauren Crux. Manvi
had been one of my most engaged intermedia art students
the year before the *LINEAGE* project began, and they
became my assistant in designing and fabricating the first
exhibition. Manvi's mixed-media installation was one of the
eleven featured works.

My notes remind me that I initially offered a choice of
three archived individuals to Manvi. The one Manvi selected
surprised me: Dodi Horvat, a science fiction writer of uncertain gender. In the three years I had known Manvi, I had
no idea they were passionate about sci-fi or about gender-
nonconforming identities. My first encounter with Horvat's
archive revealed a rich trove of typed and handwritten papers
along with a scattering of color photos. Horvat had a background as a microbiologist and a mycologist. The box was
filled with field recording notes on flora, fauna, and mush-
rooms, observed on walks in the San Francisco Bay area
during the 1980s, and science fiction notes and drafts for a
manuscript labeled "Amazon Sci Fi" from the 1970s. Among
the notes were doodles and sketches along with odd charts
and schematics that map out Horvat's characters and plots.

I found fanzines with titles such as *Tales of the Free Amazons*, *Starstone*, *Pandora: A Femzine*, and the *Darkover News-
letter* "Free Amazons" special issue. Another folder was labeled

"Planet Building" and contained notes for "Science and History of a Small Planet." In a separate file I found a selection of informal snapshots of Horvat with friends, printed in the undersaturated colors that mark 1970s color photography. Two cassette tapes contain three interviews with transgender men, including the transgender activist and author Jamison Green, all conducted by the friend who donated Horvat's papers to the Historical Society in 1997, Thyme Siegel. Horvat was also active in the Gay and Lesbian Sierrans, Options for Women Over 40, and the Lesbians Over 40 Rap Group of Options.

Amid all the documents and ephemera, it was difficult to find basic biographical facts. Not much is revealed about Horvat, apart from their residence from 1967 to 1989 in San Francisco, where they began to create this science fiction odyssey in thirteen handwritten notebooks. Sections of the notebooks contain extensive material about the culture, politics, geography, religion, and populace of an intricately envisioned world, complete with population statistics; descriptions of dozens of planets, cities, political parties, rites, myths and creation stories; and maps and drawings of characters and places. Horvat's Amazon is a clan-based matriarchal society in the far future, a time when gender ratios have changed to three females for every male. In notes and manuscripts, Horvat developed an original system of sexuality and gender that alludes to a personal struggle. Earlier archivists' unattributed notes give contradictory accounts of Horvat's identity, describing Horvat variously as a lesbian and a transgender man. It wasn't until I delved into the Online Archive of California that I found the date span of Horvat's life: 1940–1989.

Manvi embarked on a process of excavating the richly detailed fictional world contained in Horvat's archive and was acutely tuned in to Horvat's focus on gender fluidity, to clues inside and outside the writing that they might have identified as a male in the 1970s. In an installation that resembled a four-foot section of a stage set, Manvi created a "ruelle," an archaic term for an eighteenth-century secret bedside compartment, as a metaphor for Horvat's exploration of identity and desire. Titled *Tools for (Re)Construction/Ruelle*, this wall structure held an open drawer filled with odd hybrid tools made of wax that Manvi designed to offer Horvat a metaphorical way to re-imagine a body to suit their self-image. These bone-like artifacts, along with Manvi's elegantly hand-drawn instructional wallpaper, form a posthumous gift to Horvat, directly from Manvi's own gender-nonconforming process of change. Manvi wrote:

> A ruelle is an antiquated concept of the space between the bed and the bedside table, a closet or a cabinet that was used to keep personal keepsakes. An archive could then be read as a ruelle gone public. Ever since I began to engage with Dodi Horvat's archive, I think about it constantly. It's as if Dodi's writing and photos, in all their ambiguity, crawled their way up into my corpus callosum and carved the tissue and gray matter, making a home for themselves. I have a knowledge of what I desire Dodi to be. There is no resolution, no closure, to my relationship with Dodi. The more I try to take the material fragments of Dodi's life and reconstruct some sort of narrative, the more I find the story reminds me of myself. This uneasy and ambivalent process is oddly comforting, oddly familiar.

I was struck by how strong Manvi's connection to Horvat was across a two-generation age gap. My own connection was rooted in the 1970s, when Horvat would have been an older dyke in my San Francisco world. The faded photos in the archive show Horvat alone and with clusters of friends, all of whom look like people I might have known. I scanned these photos repeatedly, thinking I might recognize someone. This connection made the mystery of Horvat's life seem tragic, especially since nothing in the box indicates how they died at the young age of forty-nine.

Now, twelve years later, Manvi recalls spending considerable time with Horvat's journals, texts that were filled with sci-fi world building and insight into characters for novels, notes that appeared in margins or between unrelated to-do lists and appointment times.

Looking back, I don't actually know if Dodi was as preoccupied with gender as I imagined (or wanted) them to be. I often experienced the process of looking through an archive as untethering. Without any sort of formal schematic or guide, I tended to wander, unmoored. The moments, words, or objects I attached myself to often spoke more to what I wanted than to Dodi. So, it's no surprise that I latched onto how Dodi wrote about gender. With all the cartwheeling they did in their writing to try and circumvent the constraints of gender, I remember feeling like they found the problem as vexing as I did. Dodi's characters could move between genders, shed them if necessary, and morph into specific genders for different tasks. It seemed to me like the short shrifted-ness of their body disallowed them from experiencing masculinity in its fullest dimensions.

I remember often feeling guilty and irritated while looking at Dodi's archive, like I at once didn't know them and was leering at something that was theirs, unnamed and therefore precious. It was from that place that I started trying to look for a concept that was the opposite to archiving, but still held a relationship to material. When I happened upon the construct of the ruelle, it felt like the right bit of space I wanted to carve out with Dodi.

I also remember going on a hike in the redwoods with my friend Pascal a week or two before I flew to Texas to have top surgery. I spent much of that hike nervously grilling Pascal about his memories of surgery and his feelings about his body's current iteration. In one frozen moment, we were looking out onto the bay when Pascal turned to me, smiling, and said "but, Maya—our bodies are changing all the time, with or without our consent. How wonderful is it that you get to decide? I remember telling myself before I got the surgery, that if one day down the line I ever became a woman again, fantastic, I'd be a woman with a beard and no tits." I think about that moment all the time. It reminds me how fruitless and wonderful it is to tend to your choices around gender. Before surgery I thought there was going to be an acute "before," and that I would be living in some type of new "after," where, without tits, I would feel full of self-determined certainty. It has been a pleasant surprise to experience an ebb and flow, rather than a cleave. I rarely ever think about Dodi, or their archive. But . . . I rarely ever think about the moments in my life that I was certain were definitional, rather than what they turned out to be— transitional. So, in that way, Dodi is incredibly important to me.

Manvi, who was my student when this project was in its embryonic phase, has since become a good friend. We communicate, laugh, and bond from the vantage point of different genders, different racial ethnicities, and a forty-year difference in age. I slip up on pronouns, even as I learn how that hurts. We talk about politics, culture, and history, and each time I am newly surprised by how interested they are in my history, my queer trajectory. Our collaboration has extended beyond the *LINEAGE* project to encompass working together on the editorial board for Q+ Public, the small book series that includes this book.

Elissa Perry,   Pat Parker,
b. 1970   1944–1989

Mouth to Mouth, mixed-media bed installation; 2010

When I matched the writer, activist, and culture worker
Elissa Perry to the poet Pat Parker, I broke my most basic
project rule: to use archives I found in the GLBT Historical
Society collections. Parker's name popped up in several
locations within these archives, including in a 1986 video of
Black lesbian author Audre Lorde reading at the San Francisco Poetry Center. I was particularly eager to locate materials on Parker because I vividly remembered hearing her
read poems like "For Straight Folks Who Don't Mind Gays
but Wish They Weren't So Blatant." Her poems had a powerful impact on my young lesbian awareness when I moved to
San Francisco in the mid-1970s. Once, while waiting in a
long line for the women's bathroom at a concert, I recognized
Parker ahead of me. In the midst of our knees-pressed-
together impatience, she started organizing for efficiency.
Walking back and forth along the lesbian queue, she prompted
our vigilance to the progress of the line: "Watch for someone
to exit, prepare to unzip your fly" and other time management tips. It was hilarious. Parker was our sexy butch drill
sergeant, and we gladly stepped in line.

It was disappointing to find out there was no collection
specifically dedicated to Parker, but in keeping with my desire
to diversify the archives, I decided to use this as an opportunity to gather materials in hopes of creating an archive for
her. At a monthly meeting of the GLBT Historical Society
Women's Group, I learned that Parker's family, twenty years
after her death, was still holding on to her effects as they
waited to secure a commitment from a trustworthy institution
that would provide generous compensation to Parker's two

daughters. I wondered if my inclusion of her in the *LINEAGE* project was inappropriate. With some uncertainty I approached an old friend, Perry, to ask if she was interested in this match. Her passionate response sealed the deal, and I trusted that Perry would approach this project with respect for Parker's family.

Parker's story began in Houston, Texas, in 1944. In her 1978 poem "Womanslaughter," Parker describes her family:

> . . . of the four
> daughters of Buster Cooks,
> children, survivors
> of Texas-Hell, survivors
> of soul-searing poverty,
> survivors of small-town
> mentality.[5]

This poetry collection was written in response to the murder of one of Parker's three sisters, Shirley Jones, by her husband. In 1962, Parker left Texas after her uncle died while in police custody and a young boy in her community was murdered by a mob for being gay. She headed to Los Angeles to study at a community college. At the age of eighteen, she found herself in an abusive relationship with the playwright and Black Panther Ed Bullins. During their marriage, she miscarried after he pushed her down a flight of stairs.

Parker came out as a lesbian in the late 1960s, after a brief second marriage. The liberation she felt in finally embracing her sexuality echoes forcefully in her poem "My Lover Is a Woman," which uses an interracial lesbian relationship as a way to talk about racism, poverty, and the prejudice that operated within the LGBT community. This direct address about race in relation to sexuality was unusual at the time. Parker also immersed herself in socialist theory and community organizing. Her political engagement coincided with the development of her writing practice. By the late sixties, she was involved in the women's rights, gay rights, and civil rights movements and was living openly as a lesbian, writing poems, and teaching creative writing workshops. At a time when the Black Liberation Movement was laced with homophobia and misogyny and white feminists were too often unwilling to confront their own racism, Parker dared to openly hold her communities and allies accountable for hypocritical behavior.

By the 1970s, Parker had published five poetry collections with independent feminist presses like Diana Press and founded the Black Women's Revolutionary Council and the Women's Press Collective. It was during this period that her friendship with Lorde flourished. With Parker living in Oakland, California, and Lorde in New York, the two shared a lively correspondence. They sent each other advice about monetary support and writing opportunities and words of encouragement, along with photographs, magazine clippings, and—later—tips for how to ease the nausea of chemotherapy. Both Black lesbian poets, mothers, and activists provided each other with crucial forms of support and inspiration as they each battled breast cancer. Their letters were published in a book titled *Sister Love: The Letters of Audre Lorde and Pat Parker 1974–1989*.[6]

Along with other lesbian feminist poets, Parker helped organize regular poetry readings up and down the West Coast. In 1985, she worked with the United Nations, traveling with delegations to both Kenya and Ghana, and testifying about the status of women. Parker's day job was as the director of the Oakland Feminist Women's Health Center, where she worked for a decade, resigning in 1988 due to her advanced breast cancer. Parker died in Oakland on Juneteenth (June 19), 1989, at the age of forty-five, and was survived by her partner, Marty Dunham, and her two daughters.

I met Perry in 1990 when she was nineteen and a publishing assistant for *OUT/LOOK: National Lesbian and Gay Quarterly*, the journal I helped found two years previously. Recently arrived in San Francisco from the Midwest, she was a smart and charismatic Black baby dyke, who we were thrilled to bring onboard. Perry, it turns out, had encountered Parker's poetry at the age of fifteen on the bookshelf of a family friend. Starting with the groundbreaking collection of poems *Movement in Black*, she immersed herself in Parker's writing, which she credits with helping her come out. When she learned that Parker died just eighteen days before she arrived in San Francisco in 1989, Perry was heartbroken. Two decades later, eager to revisit this period of her life as a participant in the *LINEAGE* project, she embarked on a mission to discover as much as she could inside and outside of the GLBT Historical Society archives. Though her attempts to contact Parker's family were unsuccessful, Perry was able to explore artifacts of Parker's in the private archives of Oakland-based archivist, collector, and curator Lisbet Tellefsen. Perry also gathered her own books and leaflets by and about Parker, poring over them to inform her response to Parker's life and work.

Though primarily a writer, Perry explored her connection with Parker by creating an art installation. Immersing herself in Parker's life brought back powerful memories of the impact Parker's poetry had on Perry's young identity as a Black lesbian. She recalled taking *Movement in Black* to bed with a flashlight after saying goodnight to her parents, hungrily devouring the poems under her covers. Perry was compelled to seek out other works by Parker and found poems like "Sweet Jimmy" and "Womanslaughter," which left indelible marks on her memory and guided her art process in response to "the godmother or favorite Auntie I never met." She dug out her fifteen-year-old journals from a trunk in her closet and revisited her own writing from that period. She collected every book and poetry reading flyer, every reference she could find, generating a small archive dedicated to Parker. The physical form for her installation was a mattress on the floor, which evoked Perry's bedroom at age fifteen. The cream-colored sheets, on which she inked poems from her teenage journal entries, were turned down neatly to reveal books, flyers, and diaries, all available for viewers to examine and touch. And to do so required getting down on the floor, becoming a voyeur examining the two lives that converged in Perry's mixed-media art installation, *Mouth to Mouth*, which became part of the second *LINEAGE* exhibition.

Having found community, support, and inspiration in my early lesbian days through the prose and poetry of Parker, Lorde, and Judy Grahn, it was inspiring to hear about the profound impact of Parker's words on Perry. I think we each had our respective crushes on Parker, first as a living poet and later as a courageous elder. In the years since Perry created her installation, she says Parker remains "a teacher, a guide and an ancestral adviser to conjuring a new world and living the principles of that new world in this one."

Out
somewhere
and back again

Stockwell, Nancy

Camille Norton,
b. 1954

Nancy Stockwell,
1940–1999

"Breath," a poem; 2009

Camille Norton was also seated at the table for *Affair-on-the-Green* in 2008. She came the furthest distance—from Stockton, California, where she is professor of English at University of the Pacific. Her previous visit to the University of California, Santa Cruz, was in 2005 as a guest poet at Porter College, where she read from her National Poetry Series award-winning collection *Corruption*. Norton and I first met in 1994, the year we both began our academic careers. Though we were at very different kinds of institutions—Norton's a small private one, mine a public state university—our friendship developed into an important mutual support system as we navigated the vagaries of academia. We shared our creative work and talked about the benefits and pitfalls as artists in educational systems geared to scholarly writing. I found Norton's poetry powerful and had no doubt she would be among the individuals I invited to participate in the *LINEAGE* project.

While we were exchanging ideas one day in 2008, Norton spotted the name Nancy Stockwell scrawled in my notebook. Startled, she said, "I know her!" Seeing Stockwell's name revived memories from Norton's life as a young lesbian in Boston and later in graduate school at Harvard. Her personal connection fueled a palpable urge to delve into Stockwell's archive, which made my rule about participants not knowing their archive match suddenly seem too rigid. At the GLBT Historical Society, a reference to Stockwell's archive had caught my interest, too, despite its physical location elsewhere.

In early 2009, Norton came to San Francisco to find Stockwell's archive in the collections housed at the James C.

Hormel Center, which is part of the San Francisco Public Library Main Branch. There she found Stockwell's life contained in two standard archive boxes, one oversize flat box, and one document case—in the mathematics of archives, 2.5 cubic feet of shelf space. She pored over the extensive correspondence, subject files, diaries, and writings. To her utter surprise, Norton found two postcards she had written to Stockwell, in a folder labeled "Norton, Camille, 1992–1993." To see her own handwriting in Stockwell's archive, to read her own correspondence to an acquaintance who had died ten years before, made Norton realize that she had mattered to Stockwell, who had been close to Norton's former partner Jane Picard in the 1970s.

In the early 1990s, Stockwell visited Picard and Norton in Jamaica Plain, Massachusetts, the Boston neighborhood that is home to a significant community of lesbians and people of color. This was the only time Norton met Stockwell, but she remembers enjoying her company and feeling connected through writing and through parallel experiences in lesbian communities. Stockwell had been a founding mother of the journal *Plexus*, a San Francisco Bay Area feminist journal published between 1974 and 1977. Norton had published work with a Boston feminist newspaper, *Sojourner*, which had also flourished in the 1970s. Norton and Stockwell shared a lineage of second-wave feminism energized by writing and publishing for women. A number of important journals were launched in this period, including *Conditions*, *Sinister Wisdom*, and *Trivia*: *A Journal of Ideas*.

Stockwell wrote short stories and a novel but was never widely known as a writer. Included in her archive is a tough personal letter from well-known Canadian lesbian novelist Jane Rule that must have been discouraging; it describes Stockwell's writing as sloppy and not strong enough. Stockwell's legacy was forged around her role in the lesbian publishing boom of the 1970s, a period of literary DIY innovation across the country, which showcased the poetry of Audre Lorde, Adrienne Rich, Pat Parker, Judy Grahn, Cherríe Moraga, and Gloria Anzaldúa, among others. Publishing houses and collectives, including Naiad Press and Kitchen Table Press, were founded during this fertile period of gay and lesbian literature. When Stockwell visited Norton and Picard, literary passion was a strong point of connection.

Looking through the correspondence file in Stockwell's archive, Norton found other familiar names: Sandy Boucher, a leading Buddhist teacher; Ann Stokes, a friend to both Stockwell and Norton and founder of one of the first artist residencies for women in the United States; Firebrand publisher Nancy Bereano; Naiad Press founder Barbara Grier; the writer and producer Ann Meredith—threads of the lesbian literary web of the eighties and nineties made visible in the archive index. Norton also discovered correspondence with such notables as Dorothy Allison, Jane Rule, Adrienne Rich, Eudora Welty, Minnie Bruce Pratt, Kate Millett, Susan Griffin, Tee Corinne, and Margie Adam. In the process of researching Stockwell, Norton uncovered her own lineage as a writer in the world of lesbian feminist publishing.

Norton had another link to Stockwell: Stockwell was very ill with cystic fibrosis, and in the early 1990s she was on a wait-list for a double lung transplant. Norton described her distress when Stockwell would leave the room as a wet hollow hack erupted. Norton, a heavy smoker with her own hacking cough, felt a deep personal concern as she thought about the question of breathing and respiration. Soon after their meeting, Norton sent the two postcards found in the archive, inquiring about Stockwell's health, sharing friendly news, and writing how nice it had been to visit with her.

For the *LINEAGE* project, Norton immersed herself in researching the mechanics of breathing, and the grasses in Kansas, where Stockwell was born and died. She thought about a writer's frustration with productivity and audience, empathizing with Stockwell's thwarted satisfaction as a writer. The end result was a poem, "Breath," an elegy for Stockwell, who literally searched for breath in the final years of her life.

Norton wrote in 2009: "She was vibrant, charismatic and brave, with a terrible deep cough that scared me because I was then a devoted cigarette smoker. My poem speaks to the process of waiting to find a way into a poem about Stockwell, in other words, the difficult process of writing a poem worthy of her. The poem is about the two of us, poet and subject, and the topic of breath in poetry and in life."

During her life, Stockwell zigzagged across the country more than once. After graduating from a University of Kansas master's program, she moved to Boston and began her career as a writer. The unpublished novella "Lucky Girls" chronicles her time there as a high school teacher in the early seventies, her work as an editor at Arthur D. Little, and her position as an administrator at the Girls Club in Lynn, Massachusetts. In 1973, Stockwell moved to Berkeley and founded the journal *Plexus*, then five years later returned to the East Coast, where she self-published her book *Out Somewhere and Back Again: The Kansas Stories*. In 1979, she attended the first gay and lesbian march in Washington, D.C.; by 1980, she was managing the Lambda Rising bookstore in Dupont Circle and became a delegate to the Democratic National Convention. Most astonishing, given her lung disability, in 1985 Stockwell was admitted to the Ladies Professional Golf Association and returned to the West Coast to become the first female golf club professional in San Francisco. And she kept writing, with a story published in the Cleis Press collection *Best Lesbian Erotica 1996* and a reading of another piece, "The Telling Kind," at the February 1996 OutWrite conference in Boston.

These biographical markers suggest points of crossing in my own connection to Stockwell. I lived and worked in the Boston area in the same period she lived there. Like her, I attended the national LGBT march on Washington in 1979 and I remember visiting Lambda Rising, the bookstore that Stockwell managed. This palimpsest of our lives, meeting but not meeting, gives me a sense of missed opportunity. I, too, attended the 1996 OutWrite conference, my first return to Boston in years, though I have no recollection of hearing Stockwell read on that cold Boston winter day. I didn't know Stockwell, yet she feels familiar in death, another ghostly visitation as I write this book. Now I see her through Norton's research and writing, a strange kind of inhalation of the mystery of one person's life.

Back in the archive, Norton ran up against a restriction: a box labeled "Series 5" was closed to researchers until the year 2060. What secrets required sixty-one years to safely reveal? I was dying to know. Norton speculated that the restriction was put in place to protect lovers and friends until they, too, died. "Nancy had a lot of lovers," she said. In the Online Archive of California, I read that her early journals from the 1960s through the 1980s were destroyed by family after her death.

I asked Norton for her thoughts now, a decade after connecting to Stockwell through her archive:

My poem, "Breath," for Nancy Stockwell, is an elegy for a lesbian writer who died young, at 59. In the ten years since that project, I have lost friends in swift succession, among them Jane Picard, who introduced me to Nancy all those years ago in our apartment in Boston. When I read the poem now, I respond to it as an elegy for a generation of women who danced with me during my own coming of age in a gang of sexy, edgy lesbian artists. Many of us became college professors for a new milieu of radical students who identify as gender-queer and gender non-binary. Now more than ever, I value the archives of ordinary people who help us reconstruct the culture of those last decades of the 20th Century, which is, for better or worse, my century. I recently reread Nancy's book, *Out Somewhere and Back Again: The Kansas Stories* (1978), and took note of the strong talent evident in her fiction writing. If I have a wish for her, it is that she will discover dedicated mentors in her next incarnation as a wordsmith.

BREATH

The poem she wanted was waiting for the next breath.
She wanted to push it like a girl on a swing.
Into the line and out again,
into the line, out into

    switchgrass rippling across the prairie.

How long would it wait, she wondered?
Would it wait longer than the gasp between lightning
    and thunder?
How long would it hold its breath in defiance of her?

She decided to make a study of it,
of breath that originates in the mind.
Not in the mind, exactly, but in the brain's
beautiful pith, in the long and narrow
starry shadows of the medulla.

Inside the starry shadows are two kinds of breath:
voluntary and involuntary, like armies and lovers.
There is the breath one masters.
And the breath one is mastered by.

But which was the breath that would master the poem?
And how would she know it when it arrived?

Would it be a minstrel breath out of Kansas,
climbing out of her fiddle?
Or the strict churchy music of childhood
lifting up from a steeple into the trees,
some long ago meter that used to mean
you'd go to heaven if you were good.

If she was good, why couldn't she breathe?
If she could breathe, the poem would go to heaven
the way a girl on a swing heaves away from the earth
     with a force.

When it came finally, the breath was sweet and dry
as the desert in spring.
The poem sounded like shush, shush, shush.
Then the clatter of wind and something half-heard,
like laughter and an old-timey voice

singing: *Something's wrong with Miss Nancy.*
She won't say and I can't guess.
Dying, probably for lack of a prairie
or is it breath?

Gabriella Ripley-Phipps,
b. 1987

Sally Rosen Binford,
1924–1994

The Archival Dinner Party, participatory event,
mixed-media installation; 2009

Sally Rosen Binford's fascinating history touched the lives of several people I know. Though her artifacts are not among the holdings of the GLBT Historical Society, she makes appearances in several organizational archives, including the San Francisco Sex Information records. Following my urge to find out more about her, I challenged Gabriella Ripley-Phipps, one of my senior art major students, to build an archive for Binford, and I put her in touch with the people who could help.

"Sexpert" writer Susie Bright was close friends with Binford, as was Bright's former partner, the photographer Honey Lee Cottrell. In a blog entry shortly after Binford's death by suicide, Bright wrote: "Sally was an astonishing person. A pioneering anthropologist and archeologist, her writings on prehistory are required reading for most college courses in those disciplines. A passionate antiwar activist who dropped out of academia at the height of her career in the 1960s, she was one of the founding mothers of the modern feminist movement, a charter member of N.O.W. [National Organization for Women]. But beyond that, she was the first woman ever (if you don't count Emma Goldman) who I'd call the very model of a sex-positive feminist."[7] It turned out that in addition to her professional accomplishments and her pivotal work as a feminist, Binford had lovers of all genders, held monthly dinner parties at her house, and participated in a regular poker group. After leaving her respected career as an anthropologist, she became the only bisexual organizer of the first Conference of Old Lesbians held in San Francisco in 1989. I imagine she must have sat in meetings with Janny MacHarg, another subject of this project, who was also involved in this seminal conference.

Ripley-Phipps immediately contacted Bright, who helpfully steered her to Binford's granddaughter as well as to members of Binford's poker group. Ripley-Phipps attended a meeting of the poker group and followed up every other lead that presented itself. In the early stages of her research, Ripley-Phipps described not feeling close to Binford, saying she felt more connection to the friends and family who loved her. Ripley-Phipps wrote: "I don't like her. If only I could understand her need for control, if only I knew why she loved poodles, if only I knew why she and her daughter were not close. I see many sides of Binford that were bright and brilliant but get no understanding of her darkness."

Ripley-Phipps persisted, intrigued by the stories of Binford's famous dinner parties, which inspired her to create her own performance dinner party. For this event, Ripley-Phipps invited eight fellow students as guests and instructed them to imagine five objects they would leave in an archive. It was a novel experience for people in their early twenties to discuss what would happen after they died. Most had never thought about legacy or what they might leave behind. Ripley-Phipps described her event:

> I cooked a pasta dinner and set up a fancy table in E. G.'s
> campus art studio. I led each guest to a box with the
> anonymous objects another participant had chosen and
> gave each a clipboard with a survey. They answered
> questions about the person whose items they were looking
> through, questions about the person's favorite color, about
> their relationship with their parents, the age of their first
> kiss, their hopes and dreams. I then sat them at the table,
> with the person whose box they had examined to their

right and the person who explored the box they had compiled to their left. As we ate, I instructed them to turn to their neighbors and to investigate who that person really was, to get answers for the questions on the survey. The piece was inspired by Sally's practice of throwing raucous and exquisite dinner parties (that often led to orgies). Mine included no orgies but instead explored what I had encountered during my process of creating Sally's archive, the difficulty of ascertaining who someone is through objects, through interviews, through documents. My participants had a chance to push back against the projections of the others as I was not able to do with Sally.

For the first *LINEAGE* exhibition, Ripley-Phipps created a compelling mixed-media installation. Eight clipboards hung on the bottom half of steel archive shelves, each one displaying one of her participant surveys. Ripley-Phipps attached a grid of nine archive boxes to the wall, openings facing out and positioned catty-corner to the surveys. The center box held a video monitor that played a loop of the live event; the other eight boxes held the artifacts donated by the participants in Ripley-Phipps's dinner party. The materials related to Binford, which Ripley-Phipps gathered with the help of donors like Cottrell and Binford's granddaughter—photographs, brochures, and event notices—became a new archive at the GLBT Historical Society.

Binford was a lively and creative activist from an earlier era. As a divorced single mother in the 1950s, Binford endured grueling sexism in her journey to become an archeologist and anthropologist. Often criticized for her tight sweaters and makeup, she wore a jacket to archeological digs adorned with the words "I'm not here to cook, I'm here to dig." In graduate school, she met Lewis Binford, who later became a renowned anthropologist and her third husband. As a team, they co-founded what became known as the New Archaeology, an influential movement that promoted a more scientific and quantifiable approach to the field. Though Sally Rosen Binford was instrumental from the start, she rarely got credit. Liz M. Quinlan, a graduate student at the University of Massachusetts, Boston, described this slight in a presentation at the Society for American Archaeology in 2019. Her paper's title, "'. . . and His Wife Sally': The Binford Legacy and Uncredited Work in Archaeology," sums up this all-too-common pattern.[8]

Susie Bright, in a 2008 online journal entry, includes extensive excerpts from an interview with Binford that author Janet Clinger included in her book *Our Elders: Six Bay Area Life Stories*. Binford described teaching at the University of California, Santa Barbara (UCSB), with her husband, Lewis. She experienced openly anti-Semitic comments from colleagues in the anthropology department. "I made a great point of signing myself Sally Rosen Binford. I also made a point of speaking a few words of Yiddish at the faculty gatherings."[9] Other attitudes toward racial and ethnic minorities added to a tense atmosphere at the school. The department was recruiting anthropologists with expertise in Native American and African cultures to come to Santa Barbara. Binford knew a Native American scholar and activist and a distinguished Africanist and recommended them for the positions. After one faculty meeting, the chair of the department remarked, "Doesn't she know any white people?"[10]

Binford left UCSB, anthropology, and Lewis Binford in 1969. But her life of protest was far from over. Binford participated in the civil rights movement starting in the early 1960s and the anti–Vietnam War movement (for which she used her academic influence to shield students from the draft) and became a charter member of NOW. In the early 1980s,

Binford joined forces with the Gray Panthers, a multi-generational advocacy network that challenged ageist laws and discrimination. She also joined the board of Community United Against Violence (CUAV), an organization founded in 1979 following the assassination of Harvey Milk, the first openly gay elected official in the history of California.

In 1978, Binford moved to San Francisco, where she became fascinated with the Bay Area lesbian scene. While there, an essay she published stirred up considerable controversy. In "Myths and Matriarchies," she argued against the mother goddess movement of the 1970s and 1980s that believed prehistoric groups in antiquity were matriarchal, peaceful, and egalitarian, led by women who worshiped earth goddesses.[11] Binford challenged this interpretation, asserting that there was very little hard evidence of a pervasive goddess culture in prehistoric Europe and the Old World. She critiqued the use of myth as history, refuting it as appropriate data for reconstructing the past. This drew heavy criticism from some feminists, who declared Binford's article treasonous and accused her of being brainwashed by the male establishment. In the interview by Clinger, Binford said: "I pissed off a lot of the soft-headed feminists. . . . For them to have wasted their time on this instead of equal pay for equal work is trivializing feminism and a total waste of time. I got hate mail. . . . The focus on the former glories of the 'Matriarchy' drains off a tremendous amount of energy and interest away from current problems, like reproductive rights, equal wages for equal work, medical care and so forth, into this never-never land of what might have been in the past."[12]

Binford was a trailblazer of sexual liberation and sex-positive feminism, and her love for different types of sexual experiences didn't diminish as she aged. In her sixties, she entered what she called her "Harold and Maude" period: "I'm seeing a thirty-eight-year old man and a twenty-three-year old dyke. Also, occasional group sex parties, safe sex, of course, with old friends."[13] She volunteered as a sex educator on the San Francisco Sex Information switchboard, fielding questions about the symptoms of sexually transmitted diseases (STDs) and the best leather bars in the Castro district. "I'm their speaker on sex and aging. The gist of my presentation: use it or lose it."[14]

In the midst of this vibrant, active life, at the end of January in 1994, shortly before her seventieth birthday, Binford sent a good-bye letter to close friends, family, and lovers. She then cleaned her house, put her affairs in order, and fed a handful of pills to her old poodle, Jake, then to herself.

To those I love—

Most of you know that for some time I've been planning to check out—not out of despair or depression, but a desire to end things well. I've been lucky enough to have had a remarkable life, immeasurably enriched by the love and support of a large (if improbable) group of friends and lovers. I don't want to let it fizzle out in years of debility and dependency. I've gambled enough to know that quitting while you're ahead (or at least even) is wise.

And those of you familiar with my birthday will recognize that the timing of my exit allows me to claim as my epitaph:

Toujours soixante-neuf!
Love and good-bye,

Sally[15]

Recently, I asked Ripley-Phipps, who now goes by the name Penske, about her current feelings about Binford:

I wish I had the chance to go through the archival process with Sally again. At 33, I imagine asking her far more insightful questions than I was able to think up as a 21-year-old. I might be brave enough to reach out to her daughter to find out why they were estranged. Perhaps I did do those things and have forgotten the details of the project. Perhaps my memories have dwindled down to Sally's end and are entangled with my projections.

Especially after all this time, I am aware that my feelings are about me, my desire for elders, for mentors, my fears that I don't measure up as a queer, as a critical thinker, as a brave sex-positive adventurer. If Sally knew me, would she like me? Encourage me? Accept me as I am, in my process of healing and sorting myself out? Would she turn up her nose at me? If only I could find her birth date and cast her astrology chart! Did Sally's feelings get the best of her? Did she front self-control and confidence? Was she deeply afraid to be seen as weak, vulnerable, and dependent, and was this behind her decision to end her life?

I am aware of the phenomenon of projection, which I was so fascinated by and terrified of when I first began creating Sally's archive. I am aware of how deeply I desire connection and support from mentors, elders, and ancestors. I am aware of how my shame, shifted onto others as judgment, keeps me from accessing the support that is there. Sally, are you with me?

Terry Berlier,   H. Drew Crosby,
b. 1972   1911–1996

NFS, video, wood, MAKE controller, computer, speakers,
shutters, sensor, wires, MAX programming
by Ricardo Rivera, "Broken Appointment"
from Prelinger Archives; 2010

One of the many ideas I first had for this project was to
map the cross streets and buildings referenced in the match
archives. I wondered where the people whose lives I explored
might have crossed paths, with each other and with me.
Could Jiro Onuma have walked across an intersection on
the way to work at the Pine Street Laundry, passing Claude
Schwob on his way to the naval shipyard? Could I have
passed the beauty salon of Guy Duca (another subject of
this book) on my way to Peg's Place on Geary, a lesbian bar
where I drank, danced, and flirted during the 1970s? I wanted
to network across time, geographically imagining community and connections with these recent ancestors.

With the archive of H. Drew Crosby, I finally did it.
I recently drove to the corner of Seventh Avenue and Lake
Street in San Francisco to find the house where Crosby
lived with her partner, Marion Pietsch. All I had to go on
was an out-of-focus snapshot I took of a faded photo in
Crosby's archive that showed a 1991 garage sale she held late
in her life. It pictured the bottom half of the house, with a
narrow slice of the house next door. Just a few architectural
details and a cross street. And I found it, at 59 Seventh Avenue, featuring the same gabled arch above two doors leading to upstairs and downstairs flats. The house I walked up
to had a fresh paint job and was listed online as worth over
four million dollars. I felt a thrill to be standing before the

exact site where Crosby and Pietsch lived together for half a century.

The archive, called the Kevin Bentley Collection of H. Drew Crosby, is deceptively minimal: it holds one typed transcript of a video interview made by the writer Kevin Bentley in 1991, a few snapshots of Crosby with friends, the picture of the garage sale, and the video itself in VHS (video-cassette) format. Bentley compiled the archive and added a 1998 essay he wrote about his relationship to Crosby, who was a lesbian book collector and dealer.

I matched Crosby to Terry Berlier, an interdisciplinary artist and a professor at Stanford University. In the archive, Berlier discovered a sketchy representation of an old-school lesbian who wanted no part of lesbian identity or community. Both Crosby and Pietsch, who was a decade older, worked as police matrons at the San Francisco County Jail. After retirement, they each opened up their own bookstore. Crosby owned and operated Alicorn Books on Geary Boulevard, which sold Irish books and antiques. Pietsch's store, the Lion Book Shop on Polk, mostly contained books marked NFS (not for sale), according to Bentley. As he describes in his book *Let's Shut Out the World*, "On an increasingly well-to-do block of spacious, upper-income homes, they put up chain-link fence and a barred entry gate, to the consternation of their bridge-playing Junior League neighbors. They installed wooden shutters on the windows and every evening, Marion would sweep them closed and announce, 'Let's shut out the world.'"[16]

The piece Berlier developed in response to Crosby's archive was an interactive wall installation called *NFS*. I remember walking up to the closed shutters of a window frame with a turret peak that resembled the one arched over the entryway of Crosby and Pietsch's house. As I opened the shutters, fragments of old black-and-white films became visible, playing against a background of music and voices that seemed secretive, difficult to discern. Berlier spliced together parts of two public domain films. One was *Broken Appointment*, a 1955 educational video that tells the story of a public health nurse working in the field with a client. Crosby herself had been a nurse prior to moving to San Francisco. Berlier edited the film into a short clip to suggest a flirtatious innuendo between the nurse and her client. If the film is played to the end, the view defaults to a clip of vintage lesbian porn, which, if the viewer gets too close, reverts to the more proper educational clip. In Berlier's animated sculpture, wooden shutters became a metaphor for the fear and protection that enclosed the two women's lives. Berlier wrote about Crosby in 2010: "She was just an everyday person, no fame or extraordinariness. She was a box of contradictions, closeted and cantankerous. I wonder if she would want to be in the archive at all?"

In 2020, just days before the presidential election, I met Bentley in front of his house in Glen Park. As we stood there in our pandemic masks, he talked about a three-year period when he spent most of his Sundays with his lover Richard, helping Crosby sift through the collections of books, papers, and objects that covered every surface of the house she shared with Pietsch. In his book *Let's Shut Out the World*, Bentley wrote:

Once Marion and Drew were established on Seventh Avenue, they began acquiring in earnest: when the unfortunate Japanese were being hustled off to internment camps, Drew and Marion were there to pick over and cart home items from the hastily abandoned belongings on the sidewalks of the Fillmore. Twenty-five years later, when an ill-advised urban renewal plan demolished block after block of sagging Victorians and scattered their Black inhabitants, they bargained for the disgorged contents. When someone in an immigrant Chinese family died and, by custom, his belongings were all gathered up in a sheet and taken to the city dump, Drew and Marion followed them and rifled the deceased's effects, returning home with jewelry, fine silk pajamas, and, once, a set of false teeth, which they passed along to a toothless man they met on a bus. They referred to the dump as "the garden" in conversation, so people wouldn't know where they'd been. When Laurel Hill Cemetery was dismantled and built over, they lugged home a couple of slim pioneer tombstones and propped then against the wall in their basement, where they gathered cobwebs.[17]

Bentley told me he regretted never taking a photograph of Crosby's closet, which was filled with hangers of identical men's white dress shirts, black trousers, and men's polished black leather shoes lined up on the floor. She also carried a large jailer's ring of keys that hung from her pocket and included all the keys to the doors of the house and the chain-link fence. He told me, "She was a character and had been all her life. . . . Drew liked to assume what she called her 'Gertrude [Stein] pose,' leaning forward in her chair with one hand on her thigh like the Picasso portrait." I found an example of Crosby in this pose among the photographs in the archive.

Bentley's video interview, now in digital form, opens with the camera inside the entry of Crosby and Pietsch's home, then leads up a set of stairs to a hallway, where an old record player sits on the floor, its turntable spinning a scratchy blues song accompanied by lively piano playing. The camera view travels past open doorways revealing piles of papers and books on the floor, past two different patterns of floral wallpaper, into a room where the wooden window shutters, closed, leak bright sunlight. And there, suddenly, is Crosby in a white dress shirt, black slacks, and a black bolero tie, her pale pink skin, and her white hair swept to the side in a short bob, her substantial body a solid presence. Nearby, glass cases display an assortment of doll heads and large figurines.

The blues song ends as the interview begins, and subsequent sounds accompanying the interview consist of shrieks and squeals from Crosby's cockatiel, Alberta, and the jangling of dog tags around the neck of her poodle, Maxie, who eventually clambers up onto her lap. Bentley is mostly out of sight asking the questions, while Richard operates the camera they rented for the occasion. Crosby regales viewers with stories of a tomboy childhood and misbehavior that her father seemed to lovingly tolerate. When she was eighteen and a freshman at St. Vincent's Hospital School of Nursing in Manhattan, she was expelled for sleeping with other girls, caught when Sister Ursula discovered her in bed with a senior. One of the Jesuit priests, Father Rudke, told Crosby's father that "as far as any cure, it's much harder to straighten out women than men." Her parents took her to a doctor in New Jersey, who diagnosed her as having a "congested uterus" and prescribed weekly electrical treatments from a gadget that would send mild shocks to her abdomen. Crosby laughed raucously while recalling the ineffective treatment.

She transferred to the Phillips School of Nursing at Beth Israel and finally became a nurse in the mid-1930s. In the video, she credited her teacher, the doctor George

W. Henry, with steering her toward psychiatric nursing. He told the students that the field they chose would determine their personality, that psychiatric nursing was a form of masturbation. Henry is a familiar figure to me, as he is the author of a worn black book with a three-inch-wide spine called *Sex Variants: A Study of Homosexual Patterns*, which sits on my bookshelf, from a period when I collected old manuals and textbooks about sexuality and perversion. Sure enough, on page 1078 in the appendixes, right before a series of drawings of deviant vulvas, uteruses, clitorises, penises, and erect nipples, the physician and illustrator Robert L. Dickinson notes that "strong sex urge and oft-repeated and very active congestions are supposed to produce cervical catarrhs and chronic inflammations"—consistent with the New Jersey doctor's diagnosis.[18]

Crosby's charm, wit, and faults emerge in equal measure throughout the interview, which, as I write this, I am watching for the first time. Her racism is apparent in several anecdotes, which Bentley alluded to in our talk as he described Crosby and Pietsch's collecting patterns, their seemingly oblivious opportunism in snapping up Japanese American, Black, and Chinese belongings. Bentley also described the *race* records they collected, a term coined by a record company to promote recordings of Black music to Black buyers and later to white markets. This explains the record playing at the beginning of the interview. Further into the video, I watch and listen to Crosby tell a story about her first nursing patient, who was Black; she makes her distaste palpable with a grimace and the words "I got through that. . . . I won't say any more."

When I sent Berlier a draft of this chapter on Crosby, they challenged me on my language about Crosby's racism. I had written, "Her and Marion's racial privilege and

insensitivity also showed up in their collecting habits."
Berlier wrote:

> This new information about Drew leaves me feeling
> unsettled about the archive collaboration with you and
> Crosby. I'm struggling with my connection to her. I'm
> not asking you to clean up or edit out Drew's racism,
> but rather to name what you learned about her as
> blatant racism. I see a distinction between privilege and
> racism, although these two often overlap for white
> people. While I don't expect Drew to have the racial
> awareness of our time, I feel strongly that one should
> not soften the analysis. As you noted, these chapters
> connect a complicated web of relationships, and what
> you wrote left me uncomfortable being part of what
> now, with Kevin, has become a foursome. I guess this is
> further complicated by my awareness that being white,
> lesbian and racist too often co-exists. So, I would like
> to see a more nuanced analysis in the final edit. This
> may be a good opportunity to sit with the uncomfort-
> able history of exclusion and harm in our own
> communities.

My recent connection to Bentley added unexpected
new information to the slim archive I first discovered in
2008 and then matched to Berlier. It has helped flesh out
this interesting and eccentric white woman while, at the
same time, exposing her racism. Now, my dialogue with
Berlier is opening up a larger question: How do we view
our deceased queer ancestors without the patina of nostalgia and our desire for noble antecedents? How do we
make use of both historical context and our contemporary
awareness of issues like racism to know these characters
who live on through an archive? And how do I as a white

artist address the racism hidden in plain sight? I am imagining how almost any of the archives that are part of this project could be troubled and complicated by more research, by hearing personal testimonies from the living or finding new documents and sources. And I'm thankful to Berlier for challenging me this way. When I asked them for their thoughts about the Crosby archive now, Berlier wrote:

> Originally, the only thing that connected me to Drew was a parallel between her and my Great Aunt Ceil, who both remained closeted throughout their lives. As a young queer growing up in a mostly conservative context, my Aunt was a source of refuge and support. I have dedicated some of my practice to her coming out when she was 84 to better understand her life and to offer visibility to the parts of her life that were rarely seen while she was alive. Over the past few years, my research has led me to the Ohio Lesbian Archives, where I have been parsing through material from the time of my own childhood, as I examine the subtle visibility of queer and lesbian life in a hostile context. What this chapter on Drew has offered me is actually devastating as it sheds new light on her as not merely closeted and cantankerous but also racist. This stands in stark contrast to my Aunt—while both navigated a world where it was unsafe to be out, my Aunt dedicated her life to the racially diverse public schools in the inner city of Cincinnati. So, while there are threads of Drew's existence that intrigue me still—her experiences as a tomboy, her resilience in surviving attempts at conversion therapy, and her vast book collection—I leave this project more troubled about Drew. Does

someone with a racially harmful history warrant elevating in this way? Given that my own family is mixed race, I doubt she would speak with me, if I chose to extend an invitation. Perhaps my biggest takeaway relates more to my own recent archival work, which I will pursue with a renewed desire to dig below the level of the ephemera that can bolster a false sense of connection between lives across time.

④ TOLD GAIL

⑤ ⑥ ⎯ Admark

⎯ DR. EHLENBERGER, STANFORD
⑪ moved out to Banya
⑰
⑤ ⎯ move to Holly
⑧ ⎯ move to Kaufmans

⑫ ⎯ STARTED center for special Problems

⑨
⑭ [EEA ART TIME]
⑬ [Mr. Brickers]
⑩ [Mechanical VII, Smith]
⑤ ⎯ moved in w/ mike emory

FULL
TIME

⑲

㉚

⎯ moved to Ron Stearns

⎯ moved to Mark Davies

AUG 6, THURSDAY STARTED 7 mos.
— MARCH FELT El Peak Time.

DR. Andrew Gottlieb

Ron Stoc

UPG   Sept 6, 87

One dark night I saw the light,
   streaming thru the smoke filled
      room.
Voices laughed voices sang
   the harmony of life.....
When can I come
When can I see ?
When can I be

It all begans, such a long time ago. Before I could even remember
to remember. In a flash it was over and I'm here adrift somewhere
in the future, living the now. The past is over and gone. Thank God!
The Now is continuous movement traveling through the great time
machine called the instant of Now. It works like this,
Here it comes, there it is, oops—too late it's gone, at least if
you're not quick enough.

Life is a continuous learning experience. Every thing we are
perceive affects a future perception of the coming Nows
that hasn't arrived quite yet.
The Past is more than Now out of reach. All we can
see of it is it's reflection with ever growing ripples
distorting our image until its image is unclear.

Barbara McBane,
b. 1945

Veronica Friedman,
1945–1986

"Veronica's Ghost: Queer Time and the Porous Archive,"
essay in *Art Journal*, 2013

The file was so slim and modest I almost missed it back in 2008. Sitting high on a shelf, the dark gray portfolio box was dwarfed by more substantial collections in standard archive boxes. The label, "94-1 V. Friedman, box 1 of 1," with a round green sticker marked "surveyed" and an orange one "processed," provided scant clues about its content. I'm not sure what made me reach for this box, but once I did, I stopped my general search and eagerly carried it to a table, where I could unwrap its contents. Almost immediately I knew V. Friedman's archive would become part of the *LINEAGE* project.

Six loosely packed manila folders reference Veronica Marie Friedman. The contents include meticulously handwritten charts and lists referencing gender, correspondence with "M" and with several family members, diary entries, a curriculum vita for gender identity clinics, and poetic ruminations written on napkins and paper towels. Four versions of a hand-drawn calendar note specific life events between 1945 and 1981. Amid the pencil drawings of charts and notes, a square red napkin stands out, the kind commonly found at a bar. It is inscribed with handwritten text: "It all began such a long time ago. Before I could even remember to remember. And in a flash it was over and I'm here right now traveling to the future, living the now. The past is over and gone. Thank God! The Now is continuous movement traveling through the great time in a chair called the Instant of Now. It works like this. Here it comes, there it is, oops— too late it's gone at least if you're not quick enough!"

There are other poems written on white napkins and stained paper towels, all conveying a poignant combination of despair, hope, and existential longing. As I pored over these materials, a sketchy biography started to emerge. Friedman, born as Ronald on October 15, 1945, started living as Veronica full-time in 1981. She had been married to someone named Gail—a calendar entry for 1968 reads "Met a girl I could be gentle with (Gail)." They had a son and a daughter. In 1980, they were in the middle of a divorce. Friedman referred to all three family members as lost to her. She described herself as a lesbian and referenced her first birthday as trans with the words "I am giving birth to myself." A poem from another napkin reads:

> It's a long way away and lonely in the cold but I have to
> go tonight—I just can't wait any more . . . good bye
> Good bye to the old life
> Good bye to the cold—
> I'm going to the light
> where love is warm and
> I can be me
> Thank you for the light
> dear lord. good night.

Who to match with Friedman? For the first *LINEAGE* exhibition in 2009, I included Friedman's red napkin in one of the transparent archive boxes that formed a pyramid structure near the entrance to the GLBT Historical Society gallery. In 2011, one year after the second *LINEAGE* exhibition at SOMArts Gallery, I introduced Barbara McBane, freelance writer, scholar, artist, and filmmaker, to Friedman's box, along with two other far more substantial archives. Without hesitation, McBane chose Friedman. She was immediately captivated and wrote: "The sparseness of her archive had an allure. . . . In fact, Veronica's archive—even more than most—is marked by absences and omissions, what it does not contain or explain."

Meeting Friedman set McBane on a path of thinking, researching, photographing, and writing about archives, both theoretically and in ways specific to the sketchy notes and materials in Friedman's portfolio box. The end result was a series of photographs and the essay "Veronica's Ghost: Queer Time and the Porous Archive," published in *Art Journal* as part of a section curated by Tirza True Latimer titled "Forum: Conversations on Queer Affect and Queer Archives."[19] The short pieces featured in this forum also included ones by *LINEAGE* participants Tina Takemoto, Tammy Rae Carland, and myself.

McBane's photographs, which accompanied her essay, document some of the fragile text in Friedman's archive: five of her napkin poems, a timeline chart featured on the *Art Journal* cover, and calendar entries marking key points in her life related to gender transition. Because these images are so full of words, Friedman's handwritten texts intermingle with McBane's words like a conversation. Here are excerpts from McBane's essay:

Veronica's desires resonated with aspects of my own work as a filmmaker and scholar: For many years I'd worked as a film-sound editor, and in feature film sound editing, synchronization is fetishized; enormous labor is expended on aligning voices and bodies. I'd also written a dissertation on how asynchronous sound—sound not aligned with the visual image—has been used throughout film history to give voice to resistant forms of knowledge and queer subject positions. In Hollywood code-era movies, it was not unusual to connote queerness through what you heard but didn't see—often in ghost or supernatural stories about forces from the past coming back to disrupt the present. Veronica's life project was about correcting a misalignment that created a personal crisis for her. It told a story of desynchronization and resynchronization.

Also, temporal complexities and ghostly themes reminded me of archival work itself, which deals with time and memory. What we find in an archive often seems "out of synch" with the present: to issue from somewhere beyond the archive. The effect is uncanny—like the unexpected appearance of a ghost.

. . . Interleaved among her intimate writings are numerous pages from a monthly planner that chronicle her journey in an ostensibly linear fashion, but proliferate, squirm, and squiggle into decidedly nonlinear forms. The tensions between poem and list, domus [personal] and arkheion [public record] were traumatic for Veronica. And they signal a change in emerging understandings of gender and sexuality in the late 1970's.

One folder held a small collection of poems written on paper napkins that were thin and fraying. The napkins reminded me of clothing—the delicate dresses and "underthings" Veronica coveted and wanted to wear. Sometimes the napkins were spotted with ink and seemed to evoke a mysterious personal galaxy. Some were stained with traces of food and drink, evidence of herself and her immediate environment. One was red. The napkin poetry formed a metaphor for the ephemerality of the body itself, and for the repurposing of material forms.

. . . Veronica's transition is emotionally costly, even as she realizes a lifelong dream. She often speaks of a daunting aloneness with which she may or may not be able to cope. Many of her writings address her changing objects of desire. Her sexual orientation seems fluid. She declares her love for Gail, but speaks of her sexual fantasies about being "possessed by a man." Usually, though, she positions herself as a lesbian, a woman-loving woman.[20]

In 2013, the same year McBane wrote her essay, McBane and her partner, the multimedia artist Susan Working, and I collaborated on an art installation inspired by Friedman's archive. My father, Oliver, had just died in January. As I sifted through the hundreds of notes he left behind on every surface in his apartment—word definitions, lists of plant species, sudoku number grids, sketches of plant fragments, lists of book titles—I recalled Friedman's notes. Like hers, my father's notes sometimes referenced gender in the shorthand codes of a botany notebook. I was struck by the formal similarity between their lists. Both handwritten on scraps of paper, both concerned with scientific truth, and both obsessive. Suddenly, I started to imagine Oli and Friedman in conversation, comparing notes on nature and gender and societal assumptions about both. It seemed preposterous at first, two people whose lives would never have touched. But McBane, who had lost her mother the year before, responded to this idea with enthusiasm.

The three of us created a mixed-media installation titled with a quotation from one of Friedman's notes: *"So Boring!— but Not You, Nature!" (Oliver and Veronica)*. In a kind of postmortem collaboration with my father, I made enlarged drawings based on his old botanical notebooks, representations of cells, zygotes, gametes and leaf dissections, on translucent vellum to create a twelve-foot-long scroll. We ordered hundreds of red napkins printed with Friedman's poem, a facsimile that became a visitor handout. Working built an elegant vitrine with backlit insets that illuminated on one end four of Friedman's documents and on the other a photographic grid of objects my father left behind. McBane and

I created a video projection, for which she edited a soundtrack with Nomy Lamm (another *LINEAGE* participant) singing Friedman's words and I created a visual animation in which my father's and Friedman's words dance and weave in dialogue across the screen. When I think of Friedman now, I still hear Lamm's sultry voice, solemn and haunting, singing the libretto to our fictional opera.

As part of an exhibition statement, we wrote:

> Two very different people. Oliver's archive elliptically documents the contents of a 2-bedroom apartment, dense with the objects, text, photographs and furniture of several lives and lifetimes. Veronica's archive is a small box of papers housed at the San Francisco GLBT Historical Society; it covers the years 1980–1982. Oliver was a high school teacher with a passion for Darwin, botany and the natural world. Veronica was a divorced husband with a deep sense of mission about changing her gender. . . . Veronica and Oliver were both fathers. . . . While Oliver taught the biology of gender and sexuality, Veronica turned toward medicine and biology to understand her own gender dysphoria and to change it.
>
> In this installation, we imagine the lessons from Oliver's botany studies placed alongside what Veronica knew about the complexity of gender and sexuality. . . . Veronica's gender transition was, in one sense, an embodied and very personal experiment—but one that, as a scientist, Oliver might well have understood and appreciated. Or would he? Veronica's biological life-performances messed with—or queered—the taxonomies from which many of Oliver's life-choices sprang.

The last paragraph of McBane's essay "Veronica's Ghost: Queer Time and the Porous Archive" speaks eloquently to her experience of Friedman's archive and points to a larger historical context. She suggests ways an archive like this can extend across time into the future, reaching the researchers who perhaps need its story the most.

I found what was illegible in Veronica's archive to be compelling and generative. The archive raised questions whose answers could only be imagined. The porosity of the archive extended the subject "Veronica Friedman" temporally and relationally. Veronica's documents were situated at a suggestive intersection of queer memory, queer temporalities, and fluid queer identity-production. The ephemerality, contradictions, and fissures in the archive were a prompt to flesh out a vanished, pre-AIDS moment in elusive queer suburban spaces, and to bring these into conversation with "now." The holes in the archive catapult it out of linear time, into the blurred, complicating, and asynchronous temporalities of the uncanny and the spectral. They are progenerative. They activate links between queers of different generations in different times and places: links to Veronica's postbiological families (which we can only imagine); to future archive-interpreters like myself; and to the audiences of us all.[21]

Laura Rifkin,   Jessica Barshay,
b. 1958   1940–1998

Jess Unfurling, mixed-media installation; 2010

When I first discovered the Jessica Barshay collection, it struck me as quite forbidding. In three white archive boxes densely packed with papers, there was no apparent personalia, as I learned to call items like clothing and diaries, nothing that reached out to seduce my senses, nothing that even remotely seemed personal. Prying apart the manila folders was so difficult that I gave up, and too soon, it turned out.

I had just met Laura Rifkin, an artist and writer who co-founded the Wry Crips Disabled Women's Reader's Theater in the 1980s and more recently started Fabled Asp, a lesbian disability cultural and political organization. Rifkin specifically asked to be matched to Barshay, a psychotherapist and writer who had been a close older friend. She persuasively convinced me to allow this match between friends, so I turned the Barshay archive over to her.

Through Rifkin, I learned of Barshay's struggle with invisible disabilities, ones that were often unrecognized or considered invalid inside and outside the medical community. Barshay was a pioneering psychotherapist who lived with asthma, chronic fatigue immune deficiency syndrome (CFIDS), and multiple chemical sensitivities (MCS). She practiced in the Bay Area until moving to Arizona with her partner, Judith Masur, in an attempt to improve the quality of her life in a less polluted climate. An active proponent of the right to die, Barshay ended her own life by suicide in 1998. Rifkin wrote: "Jess's suicide left behind a torn piece of fabric in the universe. I continue to stitch my needle and thread into the fibers of it, knowing that it is work I must undertake, even though it cannot be repaired."

The Barshay archive includes correspondence, personal journals, publications, subject files, newsletters, medical records, and professional papers. A considerable amount of material relates to Barshay's Jewish and Buddhist spirituality, as well as to her fat activism. One box consists entirely of journals and newsletters addressing CFIDS, MCS, and related illnesses, as well as essays Barshay wrote. Her essay "Another Strand of Our Diversity: Some Thoughts from a Feminist Therapist with Severe Chronic Illness" discusses the subjects of disability and accessibility in the women's and feminist therapy communities.[22] She refers to her illnesses as women's illnesses, so often misunderstood and ignored, and vividly describes her personal physical and emotional experience of becoming severely and chronically ill. Discussing the shortcomings in the women's therapy community's response to disabled women, Barshay describes a phenomenon she calls an "active unwillingness to know."[23]

In response to Barshay's archive, Rifkin constructed an assemblage that included a vintage Underwood typewriter; a birdcage; a small, altered book cut out of a larger copy of Victor Hugo's *Les Misérables*; an original poem typed on vintage onionskin paper; and a large paper collage. Rifkin's feelings about Barshay's suicide permeated each component. The typewriter, altered book, and birdcage were placed in three stacked transparent archive boxes. The effect of looking down through this pedestal lent the installation an ethereal aesthetic. Above the pedestal, we hung Rifkin's large collage, which included artifacts from Barshay's life, torn text fragments, two childhood photos, and overlays that were both drawn and painted. Rifkin describes her artwork as "made up of scraps that make meaning of the torn and discarded pieces of life."

Jess Unfurling became part of the second *LINEAGE* exhibition. For the June 5, 2010, opening reception, Rifkin performed the prose poem she wrote for the piece, excerpted here:

I look through your archive boxes longingly . . . hoping to catch a glimpse of you. . . . Instead, I find files and files of your academic writing. A file marked lesbian, Jewish, fat, multiple chemical sensitivity. I read your writings, listen to your tapes. I hear how early on you spoke on a radio phone interview about your intention to kill yourself if your illness progressed past the point of having a good quality of life. . . . Where are the journals with your feelings, your inner thoughts, not just your outer thinking?

You are brilliant, incisive. . . . That mind-always questioning, defying, challenging, thinking, thinking, thinking. If there is a twist in the plot you are sure to mention it. . . .

I am looking for you but I do not glimpse you. I observe pieces of your personality, interests, pre-occupations, political opinions, ideologies. I scan through the many letters sent to you, each chronicling progressive bouts of illness that others are going through. . . .

I am disappointed and angry to find you are absent in your own archive. Were you ever really here?

. . . I find a daily planner in which you document your daily losses. I am surprised to find my name in there, however briefly, and I reach in to contact you, to feel you, to touch you.

I finger the grade school class photo with all the children. Someone has drawn a circle around you to identify you. You look bright, clean, and shining here. Yet the circle around the picture makes me feel as if you were chosen, picked out somehow to suffer, even from an early age.

I close my eyes and sense you now . . . ill, lesbian, Jewish, Buddhist, playwright, author, therapist. Sarcastic, insightful, wise, biting, uproariously funny, disappointed. Headstrong, desperate, agonized, purposeful.

Who are you?

The image comes in the form of releasing. Your spirit rises to me as I carefully tear paper after paper and layer after layer into collage. You seem to take the formless form of a Buddha rising. Here you are genderless, shapeless. The long white non-allergenic cotton clothes that you wore and laundered relentlessly every day . . . seem to be flapping like robes unfurling, twisting, shifting into clouds.

You are free now. I am sure of it. I came to the archive looking for you but I could not find you. Instead, I see I am here to release you—leaving the unknown untouched.

I asked Rifkin for recent reflections, and she wrote:

I have found, with time, that I have more acceptance and release around Jessica. I still miss her a great deal, but the pain is not as sharp as it once was. When I think of Jess, I always think of her quick wit and immeasurable gifts of insight and ethical clarity. I often wonder how Jess would see things and use that to understand how to handle various situations.

If I could talk to Jessica now, I would tell her how her suicide impacted my life. While I understand that she felt committed to the right to die and did not want to live a life of increasing misery, I never thought she could understand the impact her death would have on others. I would like that to be more visible to her. I would tell her how much I missed her. I would tell her how relieved I feel that she is not suffering and how very lonely it has been to live life without her. Maybe, I would get down on my knees and beg her not to leave, selfish as that might be.

I would also love to tell her about the younger generation and what has become of the disability movement. I'd love to say to her that her legacy had somehow been passed on, but I'm not sure it has.

Dominika Bednarska,
b. 1980

Diane Hugaert,
1955–2001

TALK, spoken word performance and broadside; 2009

The archive of Diane Hugaert grabbed my attention in a special way. As I consult my old notebooks, I am struck by how many times I sketched single objects in her box, as though compelled to make a translation. While determining how this project would unfold, I made a long, embroidered flowchart on rough white cloth, sewing her objects visually into a vertical timeline that resembled a family tree. Neither the drawings nor the embroidery made it into the final project, yet they felt necessary before I invited someone to be Hugaert's match.

Lifting the lid of Hugaert's archive box revealed a ratty old straw hat with a newer lavender ribbon band. The brim looks as if something once took a sizable bite out of it, possibly a singeing flame. Underneath, I found a small package of negatives and photographs, including two images of a dyke in a wheelchair wearing the same hat in better condition. A trophy labeled "Wheelchair Race" stands upright on the bottom of the box, its gold wheelchair holding the figure of a woman with arms raised, one hand holding a golden torch. On the small dark brown pedestal, engraved text reads "10th N.W.W.B.T. [National Women's Wheelchair Basketball Tournament] 1984 Las Vegas, Nevada, 4th Place Team."

The rest of the items in the box are notebooks and folders that include personal journals, poems, letters to and from her mother, and more photographs. I found out that Hugaert was known in her activist and literary life as Diane Hugs. She was the first coordinator, a board member, and a prominent early member of the Wry Crips, a disabled women's theater group with close ties to the disability rights movement. She had worked with and advocated for people with disabilities before becoming disabled herself with multiple sclerosis

The notebooks include detailed diary entries from 1982 to 2001 chronicling her relationships, her activism, the progression of her illness, and her work to recover from childhood sexual abuse. The box also includes personal essays, poetry, correspondence, and fiction, along with Wry Crips meeting minutes, production notes, and the group's bylaws dated 1989.

As I started to read through Hugaert's journal entries and poems, the contents struck me as so vulnerable, her feelings so exposed, that I felt like an intruder. One photo shows Hugaert in a hospital bed, pulling herself up with a suspended triangle bar. The start of a poem dated November 4, 1990, reads:

> I am the stranger
> in many people's dreams
> appearing out of no where
> offering what I have to give. . . .
> No one knows my name
> few recall how I appeared. . . .

Another poem from 1990, titled "You Saw Me Standing," includes the lines

> From the time we met
> I have been in a wheelchair
> sitting
> far below your eye level
> seems silly that it's important
> that you know what I look like
> standing
> even though it was with straps . . .

A letter from Hugaert to her mother begins, "I hear your calls . . . this is a very hard time for me emotionally and I don't feel up to arguing with you." A letter from her mother reads: "I have been trying to honor your request to give you space but it is very difficult. . . . I worry and think of you a lot but then I guess I always did." A shaded pencil drawing captioned "I Can't Scream" shows eyes peering out from under a hat. Squeezed in between notebooks and folders is a form that states, "Contains private writings, please don't disturb this ___ without my consent." Indeed, I was trespassing, and, furthermore, I wanted to invite someone else into the process.

The rawness of Hugaert's writings about disability compelled me to match her with another disabled queer person, someone who would treat her highly personal material with understanding and empathy. With the assistance of Laura Rifkin, I matched Hugaert to Dominika Bednarska, slam poet, doctoral candidate, and disabled lesbian activist.

Bednarska met me at the downtown GLBT Historical Society offices after hours so that I could take a formal portrait of her with Hugaert. Darkness was essential for these sessions since my aesthetic strategy was to pose participants in the sharp glare of a projector, with no ambient light to diffuse the shadows that cut across the image. The photo session was fun and brought out Bednarska's performative skills. But what lingers in my memory even more than the session itself is her entry and our exit together. She arrived in her wheelchair, with arm braces stashed behind her seat. Her ideas about how to pose were essential, especially given my inexperience directing someone in a wheelchair. At one point, she used the arm braces to stand up and move away from the chair for a couple of poses. I raised and lowered my camera and the projection accordingly. Afterward, we exited the building together and headed toward the BART (Bay

Area Rapid Transit) station, which is underground. It was a harrowing trek for me, but I am pretty sure it was quite a typical one for Bednarska.

In her chair, Bednarska raced to push each automatic street crossing button, then as soon as the "Walk" sign lit, she darted out into the intersection with no hesitation. I was terrified cars wouldn't stop or wouldn't see her at seated level. Yet, I struggled to keep up as her electric wheels raced ahead. What slowed this three-block trip was the difficulty in finding the station's street elevator. The signs were far from clear, and the closest elevator was closed for repairs. I could hear the annoyance in Bednarska's voice and realized that this was probably not the first time she was experiencing a circuitous path to entering a train station. By the time we finally made it underground, where the trains arrived—me headed south to a stop within San Francisco, Bednarska going west to her stop in Berkeley—my nerves were frayed. I felt impatient and exhausted, both for myself and for her. This ordinary trip, at night, across the Bay Bridge, that she had agreed to do for free to participate in my project, took on another dimension. What I had so casually asked her to do seemed now like a huge and generous offer on her part.

After a couple of visits to the GBLT Historical Society, where she spent time with Hugaert's archive, taking copious notes, Bednarska crafted a conversation between the two of them. She described her process: "I'm scared to do this. I'm not sure how, what to pick and choose. What is safe to talk about, what is simply too much to take, too private, and I can't ask her for permission. . . . I wanted to construct a piece that reflected a dialogue between my writing and Diane's writing around issues of disability. I chose excerpts from her journals to respond to and combine with my own writing. I see this piece as ongoing and definitely something that can be expanded and used for performance."

Bednarska titled her piece *TALK*. Her text became a designed poster displayed in the first *LINEAGE* exhibition, as well as a spoken word performance by Bednarska at the reception for the second *LINEAGE* exhibit at the SOMArts Gallery. In this imagined conversation, she spoke directly to Hugaert: "We might have flirted if I knew you when you were alive. Now I am a kind of extension cord into the present for some kind of work or struggle or insight, and that is something that neither starts nor stops with me."

Bednarska's *TALK* was a powerful imagined conversation with Diane "Hugs" Hugaert in which she cast scrutiny on the relationship between disability and questions of what is normal. It is one part love letter across a generation and one part intervention.

Bednarska is currently unavailable to update her thoughts about her work with Hugaert's archive.

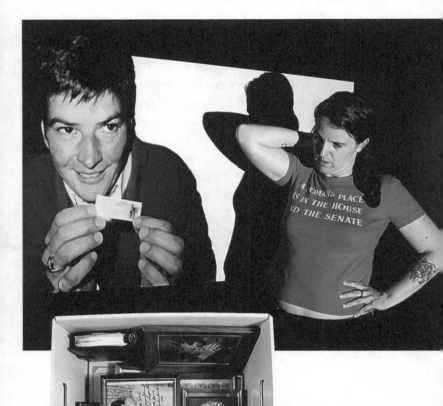

A WOMANS PLACE IS IN THE HOUSE AND THE SENATE

DEAR JO,
HERE WE ARE
IN the BACk SEAT
OF youR CAR,
IM GONNa GIVE
My LoVe to You.

DeaR Jo,
ABOUT THE PHOTOGRAPH...
AbOUT THE kiSS PHOTOGRAPH...
ABOUt THE kiss.
x X x

Tammy Rae Carland,   Jo Daly,
b. 1965   1945–1997

Jo Daly Ransom Letter 1–7, framed paper
"cut-up" collages; 2010

I matched Tammy Rae Carland, photographer, video artist,
and provost of academic affairs at California College of
the Arts, to Jo Daly, who was a longtime political and
community activist in San Francisco during the 1970s and
1980s. Daly was the first out lesbian to be appointed police
commissioner, and she served on the San Francisco Human
Rights Commission from 1980 to 1986. She was also a
longtime member of the Alice B. Toklas Gay and Lesbian
Democratic Club. During her long battle with cancer, Daly
actively campaigned for legalization of the medical use of
marijuana.

It was Dianne Feinstein who nominated Daly to the
Police Commission in 1979. Two years earlier, when Daly was
planning a commitment ceremony with her partner, Nancy
Achilles, Feinstein insisted they hold it in her garden, where
she herself officiated. Feinstein was one of the first political
candidates in San Francisco to actively court the gay vote,
even campaigning in gay bars. But her record on LGBTQ
rights was uneven and she later opposed same-sex marriage.
Daly and Feinstein clashed, and Feinstein kicked her off the
Police Commission in 1986. Daly claimed this rift was
because she once defended a porn film by James and Artie
Mitchell, a.k.a. the Mitchell Brothers.

Daly's archive is large—eleven boxes that take up 12.4
linear feet of shelf space. As I photographed each box,
I remember wondering: Who is this Jo Daly who takes up so
much space? One box holds newspapers and clippings she
collected; the newspaper on top has the headline "First Asian

on S.F. Police Commission," referring to newly appointed commissioner Tom Hsieh. Another box contains framed pictures, faux-leather-bound datebooks and a 1983 Gay Sports Award from Maud's and Amelia's, two lesbian bars. The item that fueled both Carland's and my own archive crush on Daly was an out-of-focus, faded, framed color photo that shows a passionate kiss between two women who are prone. It is clearly Daly on top, and the heat of her kiss rises up out of the box across time, into history.

The archive includes many handbill notices, such as a bright green six-panel brochure from the San Francisco Committee to Elect Jo Daly, 1974, an artifact from her unsuccessful bid for the Democratic Central Committee. She is pictured on the front panel in three-quarter profile wearing a black top, beaded necklaces, and linked women's symbols.

Several calendar datebooks are filled with the cryptic entries of a busy woman. But in the one that spans the last year of her life, there are hints of her personal struggle with colon cancer and lung cancer:

> Breathing very difficult / needed oxygen. By Sat. pm couldn't make flight of steps without stopping 2X to rest.
> Monday (today)—Abdominal pain / lost 61 lbs to 71 lbs.
> New med Naproxen, gained 10 lbs / no appetite. / abdominal pain + swelling, facial swelling.

Throughout her illness, Daly actively campaigned for the legalization of marijuana for medical use. She was quoted in her October 6, 1997, obituary on the *San Francisco Chronicle*'s SFGATE website: "'I can't explain to anyone how violently ill you can become after chemotherapy,' she said. 'You lose control. It's like a nuclear implosion inside your body. The word nausea doesn't even come close. But with the marijuana—just a tiny bit—it went away almost instantly.'"[24]

Daly was also quoted in a class action case that challenged and eventually won against the federal government's policy of punishing physicians who recommended marijuana to patients (declaration in *Conant v. McCaffrey*, February 14, 1997):

A friend then gave me a marijuana cigarette, suggesting that it might help quell my nausea. I took three puffs from the cigarette. One-half hour later, I was calm, my nausea had disappeared, my appetite returned, and I slept that evening. My use of medical marijuana had a secondary, though by no means minor benefit: I was able to drastically reduce my dependence on more powerful prescription drugs that I was prescribed for pain and nausea. With the help of medical marijuana, which I ingest only occasionally and in small amounts, I no longer need the Compazine, Lorazepam, Ativan and Halcion. No combination of these medications provided adequate relief. They also caused serious side effects that I never experienced with marijuana.[25]

In the SFGATE obituary, the journalist Sabine Russell wrote:

Jo Daly, a former San Francisco police commissioner, detective, cab driver and lesbian activist, has died after a long battle with cancer. She was 51. With her longtime friend Jill Ramsey at her side, she died at 3:15 p.m. Friday in San Francisco General Hospital. She was a favorite of the city's powerful and a defender of the powerless, and the late Chronicle columnist Herb Caen once referred to her simply as "the wonderful Jo Daly." As San Francisco's first lesbian Police Commissioner, Daly often took issue with the department she oversaw, and in particular was a thorn in the side of former chief Con Murphy. . . . Daly's short life spanned a rich and turbulent history of San Francisco politics. In 1975, she was appointed as a staff member on the city's Human Rights Commission, and at the time, was noted as the first government official anywhere whose salaried job was to serve the gay community. A native of Washington, she made a decision to announce her homosexuality publicly in 1972, after what she described as a period of reflection in a log cabin near Manassas, Va., with only her St. Bernard, Michelle, to keep her company. . . . She once told the Chronicle, "People have fears that we're always trying to convert others into a gay lifestyle. There's no need to worry. I grew up in a heterosexual environment, and it didn't rub off on me."[26]

Carland tuned in to Daly's butch sexiness right away. She created *Jo Daly Ransom Letter 1–7*, a series of seven collages that resembled ransom notes. The individual letters, all cut from magazines and glued to one side of a manila folder, spelled out messages of love and flirtation:

Dear Jo,

Here we are in the backseat of your car, I'm gonna give my love to you" and "Dear Jo, About the photograph . . . about the kiss photograph . . . about the kiss.

XXX.

These referenced the photos in Daly's archive, but they also served as a flirtatious connection across generations between Carland and Daly, who never met. The seventh framed ransom note in the series reads: "Jo, I have been told you were vivacious, loved a good argument and had a laugh that could call down the goddess. I have no doubt."

I remember Daly, though we never met. She was active in the Democratic Party, a public figure I recognized from photos in the *San Francisco Chronicle*. She was also one of the few openly gay delegates to the 1976 Democratic National Convention. Back then, in my late twenties and early thirties, I considered myself too radical to pay attention to Daly or to the arena in which she was an activist. Because she was involved in the establishment political system, especially as police commissioner, I disdained her politics. Daly's sympathy for porn, had I known, would have no doubt warmed me to her. Now with the perspective of age, I have gained respect for Daly and her legacy. While I was enmeshed in lesbian identity politics and solidarity with anti-imperialist movements, Daly took a pragmatic approach to making change in local politics, daring to be out and visible in public life. From my vantage point now, Daly was brave and accomplished a lot in her shortened life.

Carland is currently unavailable to update her thoughts about her work with Daly's archive.

Dorian Katz,   Cynthia Slater,
b. 1967   1945–1989

So you wanna do SM, huh?, acrylic and blood
on paper, 2 × 60 inches; 2010

Cynthia Slater's archive is contained in a slim, dark gray
portfolio box. The open lid reveals several copies of *Growing
Pains*, a magazine published by the Society of Janus, and a
subtitle on one cover reads "Inside: Cynthia Slater Interview." She was born the same year as Jo Daly, and I wonder
if they ever crossed paths. Slater did cross paths with three
of my friends, the photographer Honey Lee Cottrell, "sexpert" writer Susie Bright, and anthropologist and sex radical Gayle Rubin, co-founder of Samois (a lesbian feminist
BDSM [bondage, discipline, dominance and submission,
sadomasochism] organization). The late Honey Lee Cottrell,
Slater's lover at one time, created a striking photograph of
her riding naked, hair flying, on a white horse named Drummer. Robert Mapplethorpe, in his series on queer BDSM,
also made an iconic photograph of Slater in 1980, labeled
"Dominatrix woman with leather vest and exposed, pierced
nipples standing with her head turned away and moving a
large wheel."

In 1972, Slater and her boyfriend, Larry Olsen, ran a classified ad in the back of the counterculture newspaper the
Berkeley Barb for the purpose of convening a meeting to discuss BDSM. This meeting attracted ten people and eventually led to the founding of the San Francisco–based education
and support group known as the Society of Janus. The
Leather Hall of Fame biography of Slater quotes her:

> There were three basic reasons why we chose Janus. First
> of all, Janus has two faces, which we interpreted as the

duality of SM [sadomasochism] (one's dominant and submissive sides). Second, he's the Roman god of portals, and more importantly, of beginnings and endings. To us, it represents the beginning of one's acceptance of self, the beginning of freedom from guilt, and the eventual ending of self-loathing and fear over one's SM desires. And third, Janus is the Roman god of war—the war we fight against stereotypes commonly held against us.[27]

In a February 1979 *Drummer* magazine article about Janus, founding editor Jack Fritscher quoted Slater: "Anyone who's a member of a sexual minority in this country, no matter how much work they've done in their head or how much external support they get, always carries a remnant of the crap that society has laid on them."[28] Slater was always critical of sexist assumptions about SM roles, and she adamantly insisted on active consent as a requirement for ethical and mutually satisfactory SM activities. Slater saw SM education as a way to promote responsible behavior in the SM community.

Slater's activism extended further: she fought successfully for women to be accepted within the gay male leather scene in San Francisco during the late 1970s by, among other things, persuading the management of the Catacombs, the most famous fisting club in the world, to open up to lesbians. Slater coined the term "SM 101" and presented safer-sex education workshops in bathhouses and BDSM clubs. In 1985, Slater, who was HIV positive, organized the first Women's HIV/AIDS Information Switchboard. She also contributed to developing and disseminating kink-friendly safer-sex technologies, created intake questionnaires for submissives/bottoms that are still widely used, led the first open workshops on SM, and was essential to bringing leather to the

LGBT parade. She was a "pro domme," a paid professional, who started the first support group for bisexual women with HIV. In 1989, Slater died from complications of AIDS, and her death is commemorated in an AIDS Memorial Quilt panel. In 2017, a landmark art installation known as the "San Francisco South of Market Leather History Alley" was created, and in it Slater is honored with a metal boot-print displaying her name and a short statement about her life.

Looking through Slater's sparse archive in 2008 made me realize what a tourist I had been in San Francisco's radical queer sex scene. I was a defender of Samois in the late 1970s when both my lover and my best friend castigated the organization as dangerous and depraved. I was a voyeur at a 1980s party in the basement dungeon of a private home and a nervous visitor to a sex club in the 1990s. And then there was my flirtation with leather: a bustier worn at the yearly pride parade on the back of a Harley, studded bracelets, a leather cap. Though I expressed thanks to Samois for liberating my fantasies, my leather was by and large a fashion statement, my experimentation mostly private.

When I introduced Slater's archive to Oakland, California, visual artist and curator Dorian Katz, she accepted the match with enthusiasm, embracing Slater as a teacher. She wrote: "Dear Devoted Gifted Matriarch of Sadism, thank you for taking me in as your mentee." After I saw some of Katz's whimsical kinky paintings full of animal protagonists, I knew she and Slater were a good match.

The painting Katz created in response to Slater's archive was larger than life. Framed like a Renaissance masterpiece in ornate gold with burgundy velvet inset, it measured five feet high and almost as wide. The only painting in a mixed-media exhibit, and positioned next to two video pieces, it held its own. In the center, Katz painted a life-size figure of a bare-breasted Slater boldly facing the viewer, left hand holding a cigarette and right hand reaching up to a rack of SM tools. Smaller figures of animals flit and play around her: a piggy humping another piggy, all legs with boots; a bat sporting a full beard with the letters "fuc" and "ker" on separate wings; ponies fucking; a reindeer fucking another creature from behind, who is in turn fucking a rabbit with a harness from behind. In a sly nod to the photographer Mapplethorpe, a rat mimics his self-portrait with a whip up his ass, a jar of Crisco nearby. It is a riotous melee of activity, fully worthy of celebrating Slater's bold and bawdy legacy.

Looking back, ten years later, Katz reflects:

> When I think about Cynthia Slater and getting to participate in your project, it becomes a story of how the simple act of saying yes to one project changed the work that came after. This led to me and my partner, Marlene Hoeber, becoming very involved with the archive and gallery program at Center for Sex & Culture (CSC). When I asked co-founder Robert Lawrence about materials related to Cynthia Slater, he invited me to search for a box in an unorganized storage space. The box of her papers was remarkable and equally so were his personal stories of her.
>
> Marlene decided to build new shelves and give a semblance of order to the storage space of the CSC. Soon after, I became CSC's gallery director and Marlene, the archive director. There was no money, just a belief that this stuff matters. I was gallery director for eight years and developed a true-to-me relationship with CSC's archive. I've even said I'm not sure where the archive ends and I begin.
>
> My painting of Cynthia now lives with Robert Lawrence and Carol Queen, the founding directors of CSC.

Robert and Cynthia were very close. So much of the sex radical history of San Francisco is tied to seeds started by Cynthia Slater—Society of Janus, The Exiles, and peer-led adult BDSM education. Through the one step of participating in E.G.'s project, I became a small piece of Cynthia's legacy.

Miki Yamada Foster,   Trevor Hailey,
b. 1984   1941–2007

Trevor Maps the Castro, mixed-media, and
Disorientating the Castro, single-channel
video; 2010

I'm not sure how I missed the experience of a Trevor
Hailey tour of the Castro district. Even though I lived
in San Francisco the entire sixteen years she led these
historical tours, somehow it slipped by me, and I'm now
filled with regret. I love walking, love walking tours, and
also love this approach to teaching the history of a neighborhood. I've signed up for walking tours in other cities
and in other countries, so why not here? Possibly, I was
too blasé about my own city and about the eight square
blocks of the Castro, where I often ate, shopped, marched,
and socialized. I now look back to this recent history,
longing for the San Francisco that has been eclipsed so
dramatically.

Hailey's archive is filled with artifacts from her famous
tours: fan mail and flyers, a scrapbook, her notes, news clippings, and snapshots. The rainbow suspenders she wore
drape casually over the row of folders and notebooks. A yellow spine with the hand lettering "Keith Haring Guest
Book" is tucked at one end. Labels appear to have been
quickly scrawled in pencil: "Cruisin' the Castro," "Tour PR,"
"Advertising," "Fan Mail," "Newspaper Clippings." One
photo shows Hailey as a young navy nurse, looking saucy
and cute in her tailored white uniform.

Born Dorothy Evelyn Fondren, Hailey grew up in Mis-
sissippi, joined the navy, and worked as a navy nurse in New
York, the Philippines, and, finally, at the Naval Hospital in
Oakland, California. In 1972, she moved to San Francisco

and began a career as a real estate agent, working down the street from Harvey Milk's camera shop around the time the gay community had begun to settle in the Castro district. Hailey also took courses in recreation and leisure as a graduate student at San Francisco State University. During a lecture by Shirley Fong-Torres, the longtime leader of Chinatown walking tours, the idea of a walking tour first came to Hailey. With a minor in history, Hailey also volunteered filing articles and ephemera at the GLBT Historical Society. As she told *San Francisco Chronicle* writer Delfin Vigil on June 16, 2007: "That's when I discovered we even had a history. Until then, I thought we'd all sprung full-bloom from rocks."[29]

In 1989, Dorothy Fondren changed her name to Trevor Hailey and created "Cruisin' the Castro," a walking tour that educated thousands of people about the history and politics of the Castro. She reportedly had a raspy southern drawl, which can still be heard in YouTube videos. In one, she jaywalks across Castro Street like a pied piper, leading seven tour takers into what she called the Castro Cathedral. Inside, a light show spotlights the astonishing ornate 1922 decor and the Mighty Wurlitzer pipe organ of the Castro Movie Theatre. In another tour, she invites eight followers to sit on a low cement bank in front of the historical landmark that was first Milk's camera store and later his campaign headquarters. It is here that Hailey narrates the tragic history of 1978, when Milk, newly elected as a city supervisor, was assassinated along with mayor George Moscone. Like any good ambassador, she's told this story as often to straight tour participants as to queer ones.

In 2010, I matched Hailey's archive to Miki Yamada Foster, a graduate student in the Digital Arts New Media Program at the University of California, Santa Cruz. Yamada Foster was in my graduate studio class her first year and later worked as a teaching assistant in my large lecture class, Tangible Memory: Artists in the Archive. Her interest in archives and mapping, and in handcraft and digital technologies, seemed perfectly suited to Hailey's method of putting the Castro on the historical map. Yamada Foster wrote:

> It felt like Trevor spoke to me through her efforts to cultivate places where people are seen, acknowledged, and loved for who they are. Through her, visitors to the Castro could appreciate the LGBTQ community as a people who have a right to historically protected space, that the history of the lives and loss experienced there is important for all to remember. This way of being struck a chord in me—a counter to the more colonizing tendency to rescript and pave over the history of places. I have deep misgivings about the ways in which the dominant culture has structured the meaning and legality of land ownership. Telling stories connects us with the wisdom and creative force of the communities who made the places we love lovable.

Yamada Foster created two linked pieces: a mixed-media painting and a video, both structured as maps. In one, she embroidered a map of the Castro with a cartoonish outline of Hailey smiling in the corner, surrounded by painted rainbows. The empty space within the map reflected the ways Yamada Foster could only make out the outlines of Hailey's life in the archive. Yamada Foster wrote: "Her visage is much like the guide in magic stories that shepherds the traveler through the unfamiliar world and acts as its liaison and guardian."

Yamada Foster's video was a parallel venture. Taking to the streets of the Castro, she re-enacted Hailey's walking tour, filming neighborhood buildings, windows with rainbow flags, and street-level shops. She was struck by all the ways the Castro had changed in just a few years and imagined this would have made Hailey sad. So many sites were replaced by what Yamada Foster calls "bullshit for yuppies." She coupled the phantoms of these sites with a mournful monologue about displacement and belonging. The coloring and the animation in the video were Yamada Foster's way of rendering what was hidden, of making a vision of what was lost come alive for the viewer.

Yamada Foster was inspired by the ways Hailey explained where people lived and worked, played and partied, and where they came together to protest discrimination and secure basic human rights. Hailey did this with details not easily found in historical records, telling how San Francisco's gold rush in 1849 created the city's first gay community; how World War II, the Summer of Love, civil rights leader Harvey Milk, and the AIDS epidemic created the heart and soul of the Castro's LGBTQ community; how Milk's arrival in the 1970s led to the creation of the rainbow flag; how the Castro became known as the "gay mecca" of the world; how many lavender cowboys there were in the 1800s; and when the first drag bar opened in San Francisco.

I was surprised to learn about Hailey's bold activism. She is credited with alerting mayor Willie Brown to the need for a rainbow flag in the Castro. Steve Adams, president in the 1990s of the Merchants of Upper Market and Castro, told the *San Francisco Bay Times*: "During a walking tour of the Castro with then Mayor Willie Brown in 1997, Trevor looked into the eyes of the Mayor and with great convincing passion said that a rainbow flag should permanently fly in the Castro."[30] On November 7, 1997, the twentieth anniversary of Milk's election victory in the race for supervisor of the Fifth District, Mayor Brown raised a twenty-by-thirty-inch rainbow flag on a seventy-foot-tall flagpole in Harvey Milk Plaza. At the February 24, 2000, City Planning Commission meeting, Hailey suggested that Milk's former camera shop at 573–575 Castro Street should hold landmark designation, and she organized others who agreed. The Planning Commission members unanimously voted in favor of the idea, and the 1897 wood structure was saved.

The Castro's rainbow flag was flown at half-mast when Hailey died unexpectedly in 2007. This was not long after she had sold her tour business and moved out of San Francisco, and only a week before the Frameline International LGBT Film Festival premiere of *Only in the Castro with Trevor Hailey*, a short film directed and produced by Rick Bacigalupi. She had planned to attend.

These are Yamada Foster's thoughts about Hailey's archive ten years later:

> In the portrait session when I posed with Trevor, I
> felt self-conscious about casting a shadow on her in front
> of the projector, and about attempting to reconcile the
> space I was taking up in telling her story. My approach to
> documentary was like this as well—through my discom-
> fort I found intimacy. But because I so rarely found myself
> on the other side of the camera, this experience felt
> shocking. I think I wanted to be able to tell stories that
> connected people in the way Trevor did, but at age 25,
> I was still figuring out how to occupy my skin and tell my
> own story. I wondered if she would find anything in my
> story resonant.
>
> I write this as I shelter in place during the COVID
> pandemic in my apartment in Brooklyn and dream of
> another time when people in the city could share space
> and touch each other. When I worked on my Trevor

pieces I was living in Oakland in a leaking slummy apartment in a place where I knew and communicated regularly with my neighbors on the block. The San Francisco that Trevor knew, pointed to, insisted on is so hard to make out under the veneer of co-working spaces. Can we imagine giving enough time to hear the stories that are going to keep our communities alive? How can we cherish something before we appreciate that we've lost it?

Trevor came off of a naval ship and saw in the city of San Francisco a place that she loved and would come to protect. I've always been attracted to and lived in cities with a history as refuges for artists, weirdos and queers. In every city I've watched the things I love like concert halls, dingy zine archives, performance spaces, record stores, multi-use spaces with mismatched furniture and volunteer punk ethos crumble and disappear and be replaced by national and international chain stores.

In the years since I worked on this project, I started working for a labor union because organizing is the only thing that makes sense to me. It occurs to me that Trevor was an organizer if there ever was one—she served as an ambassador and gave the Castro dimension and humanity.

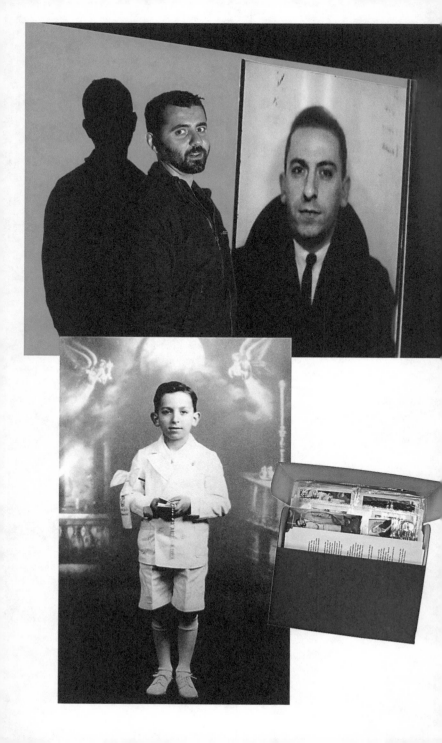

Jamil Hellu,
b. 1976

Guy Duca,
1936–1989

Making History, digital pigment print, 44 × 68 inches; 2010

I found Gaetano "Guy" Duca's archive while looking for a match for Jamil Hellu, a visual artist originally from Brazil who was completing his master of fine arts degree in art practice at Stanford University. Hellu clearly remembers his attraction to the Duca archive: "I was drawn to Guy Duca's family albums. The photographs of his childhood reminded me of my own photographs as a gay boy." Hellu felt a close connection to the Catholic references in the archive, especially in one showing Duca as an altar boy dressed in an immaculate white shorts suit, holding a rosary and looking solemnly proud. "I had a similar photograph of myself during my First Communion, also holding a rosary and the Bible. Like a mirror, I saw in Guy's archive the boy I once was."

Curious about Duca's adult gay identity, Hellu was also drawn to snapshots of him posing casually with friends while in the U.S. Navy and after. Little else is revealed in the archive. Duca grew up in Philadelphia in an Italian family. Several photos are labeled "La Famiglia Duca." In one, a man in a short-sleeved white shirt and tie tends to a woman's luxurious dark hair as she sits draped in a white smock. At her feet sits a small boy hunched over in a child-size chair, peering shyly up at the camera. Dressed in stripes, with his hair carefully parted, this little boy looks like Duca, and I wonder if this photo anticipates his future professional life. Two photographs feature obvious lesbians, comfortably posing for an unidentified photographer. They are labeled "Unidentified Friends, Late 1950's." I notice that I am happy to see lesbians in a gay man's archive.

In 1952, Duca enlisted in the navy. In his third year of service, he received a general discharge for socializing with another sailor who was dishonorably discharged on moral charges. This, of course, meant homosexual activity; Duca's discharge was based on the McCarthy-era witch hunt charge of "guilt by association," in which simply being friends with someone suspected of being a communist or a homosexual could ruin your career. While his general discharge was not as damaging as a dishonorable discharge, like many gay veterans (and all Black veterans) he received no veteran benefits. I can't help but wonder how his behavior differed from the other sailor's. Were they lovers? Was the other sailor more effeminate? Duca was only nineteen at the time, but the archive provides no clues about the personal impact of this not-quite-honorable discharge.

Duca moved in 1964 to San Francisco, where he attended cosmetology school and became a hairdresser, opening his own beauty salon on Geary Boulevard. His entrepreneurial inclinations eventually included opening a bar in the Tenderloin district of San Francisco, which suggests it may have been a gay bar. He had one business for women (the salon) and another for men. Websites devoted to extinct gay bars in San Francisco make no reference to Duca, but I wonder if his bar could have been the Milky Way on Geary, the Horny Owl on O'Farrell, or the Frolic Room on Mason. Did he cater to sailors on leave in San Francisco, looking for safe haven? Had he perhaps visited San Francisco in his own sailor days?

Duca lived in San Francisco for nearly twenty-five years, before he died of AIDS in 1989 at the age of fifty-three. In the only photo that captures him as a mature adult, he stands in front of Christmas decorations, possibly in a bar, wearing a black t-shirt with the partially visible logo "S.F.P.D." and "Pride, Compassion" circling an eagle. In this photo, Duca sports a handlebar mustache, a full beard, and the short hair of a Castro clone. He resembles so many men I knew who did not survive AIDS in those years.

Hellu decided to focus on Duca's iconic altar boy photograph, with its attribution on the back from the Roma Studio on Broad Street in Philadelphia. Setting up his own version of a formal portrait studio, Hellu transformed the small sepia-toned photograph to a life-size wall print. The dramatic enlargement brings out the backdrop behind young Duca, which is festooned with angels and an altar. In this way, Hellu rendered Duca's childhood as a larger-than-life presence. This childhood Catholic image depicting a proud family moment full of innocence contrasts starkly and poignantly with Duca's military discharge and his death from AIDS three decades later.

Hellu was also thinking about issues of queer visibility in society: "I wanted the piece to occupy a large space in the room, intersecting ideas of Guy's religious background with his gay identity. The large print represents for me the collision of both worlds in Guy's life story, his childhood religious past and his adult life as a gay man."

Working with Duca's archive had a meaningful impact on Hellu's path as an artist. He recently wrote:

Over the last decade since working with Guy's archive, my work has woven together a personal exploration of my own visibility as a queer immigrant with a deeply focused motivation to collaborate with members of the LGBTQ+ community to activate a critical dialogue about social justice and inclusion. Guy Duca's story was deeply influential in my understanding of the significance of queer archives. The stories we tell from one generation to the next help define new histories, further expanding manifestations of queer identity in the world. If I could say something face-to-face to Guy now, I would touch his hand and say *thank you*.

LAVENDER
Godzilla
VOICES OF THE GAY ASIAN PACIFIC ALLIANCE $3.00

IMMIGRATION

HOMOPHOBIA

RACISM

Vol. 4 No. 6

Troy Boyd,
b. 1960

George Choy,
1960–1993

Letter to George, framed as a broadside; 2009

In 1965, Troy Boyd's childhood was marked at the age of five when he became the first Black child to integrate his school in Meridian, Mississippi. Boyd attributes a certain shyness to this early trauma. Realizing he was attracted to other boys eventually led him to the San Francisco Bay area, where he has lived since the mid-1980s.

At the time that Boyd agreed to participate in the *LINEAGE* project, he was domestic partners with another *LINEAGE* participant, Luciano Chessa. Boyd had just been laid off from his job as a publishing administrator, so he had plenty of time to engage with an archive. It was the activism component that inspired me to match Boyd to George Choy, as well as the fact that they were born in the same year. Most of my matches have crossed generations, but I was eager to include someone like Choy, who had died so young of AIDS-related causes in the early 1990s, only a few years after Boyd arrived in San Francisco. They could have crossed paths in those years, at the EndUp on Ninth or at IBeam on Haight.

Choy's artifacts are contained in a large poster folder and in a small portfolio box that holds papers and photographs, as well as within organizational collections related to his activism. One poster for *Lavender Godzilla, Voices of the Gay Asian Pacific Alliance* shows Choy squatting in a t-shirt labeled "Queer 'N Asian," the words "Immigration, Homophobia, Racism" printed across his figure. A few photographs show Choy in sport poses, holding a ball in one picture, enacting provocative and sexy poses dressed only in a jock strap in others.

Choy was active both in gay Asian organizations and in organizations related to HIV. He was an activist for AIDS awareness and LGBT youth, a board member of Gay Asian Pacific Alliance (GAPA), and a member of ACT UP (AIDS Coalition to Unleash Power). It was Choy who persuaded the San Francisco Board of Supervisors to pass Project 10, the counseling program for LGBT teenagers in public high schools. He also worked with the Japanese Association for the Lesbian and Gay Movement (OCCUR), which brought the first gay rights case to court in Japan in 1991. And he was active in the GAPA Community HIV Project (GCHP), for which he became outreach coordinator, providing services to gay Asians and Pacific Islanders in prevention, education, early intervention, HIV case management, emotional and practical support, and direct care.

In an undated *San Francisco Bay Times* interview with Bill Lipsky, Choy said he came out to himself during the summer after he graduated from San Francisco's Mission High School, just before leaving to attend San Jose State University. He said: "I was free. . . . I no longer hid from my straight schoolmates about my sexuality."[31] He told his two closest friends he was gay, hoping they would support him, and they both did. He was best man at their weddings, and they remained confidants.

Choy saw the need for activism early on. He grew up in Chinatown, across the street from the International Hotel, a single-room-occupancy residence that was the heart of San Francisco's Philippine community. The Filipino seniors who lived there were forcibly evicted as part of so-called urban renewal during the 1970s. Their protests to save their homes and preserve their community left an indelible impression on him as a child.

In the interview with Lipsky, not long before Choy died of AIDS on September 10, 1993, Choy spoke of what he had learned since the summer after high school. "Deep inside each of us burns a special flame . . . which other people misunderstand. . . . But we, as gay and lesbian people, understand . . . that we have a special capacity to love one another. We understand that this love is real and valid. We understand that this special flame will light the way for us."[32] After his death, the George Choy Memorial Scholarship was established to support San Francisco Bay Area LGBTQ Asian and Pacific Islander students.

Spending time with Choy's archive brought Boyd into intimate relationship to Choy's committed activism. This inspired Boyd to write an emotional and highly personal letter addressed directly to Choy. Boyd described his letter:

> My letter is a thank-you to George, a reflection on life as a gay African American male in admiration of how George stepped out of the shadows and pushed for change. He made a full commitment to fostering partnerships, understanding, and awareness about AIDS, LGBT youth, ACT UP Japan and their effects on gay Asian and Pacific Islanders in America and around the world. I feel enlightened, saddened, afraid and hopeful when I look at George's life. I have read his emails, cards, letters and random thoughts, and looked at pictures of his young adult life. George faced his fears in the midst of a struggle to live. I am inspired by his curiosity to know those different from himself. George reminds me what it means to fully commit to what you believe in, to take the risk to explore the unknown through self-expression while coming to understand who he was and the purpose of his life. I found George's Act UP promotion poster to be quite bold and extremely sexy.

For the first gallery exhibition, a large, framed copy of Boyd's letter hung next to my portrait of the pair and a transparent archive box that held Choy's high school year-book and photo booth headshots encased in plastic. Here is the letter Boyd wrote:

Dear George: June 19, 2009

It is difficult writing this letter to you; how do you admit that you are attracted to someone who died over ten years ago? But there it is. I was immediately drawn to your physical beauty. Is this sick or flattering? I say it is what it is. As I reviewed your life, your Mission High yearbook class of 1978, which happens to be the same year I graduated from high school on the east coast, it made an instant connection for me. When I looked further, I came across your senior picture; you show such confidence in your senior picture that does not show in my own. Then I thought, San Francisco, the 1970's, what a great time to be young and starting your life in such a strong gay positive environment.

The environment I grew up in in Connecticut was not as positive as San Francisco. I remember watching the news of gay rallies and marches in San Francisco. I knew this would be the place where I would spend a large part of my life, as it has turned out to be. It must have been exciting as a young teen to know you had a place to go like the Castro or Polk Street to discover who you are. That did not exist for me. All I had were books, magazines, and the occasional peep show where I showed a fake ID to see two men, maybe three or more, having sex with each other. That all changed when I left home for Boston to attend college and a whole world of self-discovery opened up to me.

I continued through your archive looking for journal entries to learn what you were experiencing in your life. Sadly, you did very little recording of events in your life. On the other hand, you did record your life in pictures, which intrigued me very much. There are flyers of your involvement with GAPA, ACT UP, and the LGBT youth and a draft of a speech you gave during a special event. You started your speech: "As a gay Chinese American living with AIDS," but then you crossed out "living with AIDS"; I wonder why you deleted that statement. Maybe you were not ready or someone suggested you remove it. I'm just wondering. Your pictures show a transformation that words cannot describe. They show your insecurity with an AIDS diagnosis. They also show the strength you found within yourself, especially after your trip to Japan, which seemed to be life changing for you. This all culminated for me in your ACT UP poster campaign to fight the ignorance surrounding AIDS. It showed a strong, self-assured, determined individual finally comfortable in his own skin. I would like to thank you for your openness.

What I am trying to say is, you left a roadmap for many to follow, to take the reins and continue to work towards better medication for AIDS patients, pushing for the San Francisco youth Project 10 which is needed in every school in the United States and around the world (wishful thinking). You left such a powerful legacy that the George Choy Memorial/GayAsian Pacific Alliance Scholarship is highly sought after every year. Thank you for challenging me to look deeper into my life, to reflect on living my life as an open and honest gay African American male who meets the challenges facing the gay community today.

In Loving Spirit,
Troy

Nomy Lamm,
b. 1975

Silvia Kohan,
1948–2003

"Silvia Kohan & THE WHOLE WIDE WORLD,
a Musical Mind Meld," jam session; 2010

The five-hour jam session was held on a Sunday afternoon in an unlikely place: the large meeting hall of the GLBT Historical Society, when it was located at 657 Market Street. The third-floor room was at once both grand and funky, with off-white paneled walls, a stained wall-to-wall carpet, and four floor-to-ceiling windows that faced out to Market Street, in a building that also housed the Cartoon Art Museum, SF Camerawork, and the Catharine Clark Gallery.

The musical event was called "Silvia Kohan & THE WHOLE WIDE WORLD, a Musical Mind Meld." It was orchestrated by Nomy Lamm, a singer-songwriter and activist, who I matched to the performer and songwriter Silvia Kohan. Lamm brought together a diverse group of musicians for this afternoon session, people she had jammed with in various configurations in the past. Lamm simply put out the word and people packed up their instruments, amps, and voices and came to join her. I facilitated the space and retrieved some of the artifacts in Kohan's archive box for display, including two outfits in which she had performed. Lamm introduced participants to Kohan and taught them her arrangement of one of Kohan's best-known songs, "Spirit Let Your Love Come Through."

At first the event appeared utterly chaotic to me. As I ushered musicians to and from the back room throughout the afternoon, clusters set up their instruments in different corners, and riffs and sounds overlapped while people warmed up. As I grew more accustomed to the jam atmosphere, I became aware of the ways Lamm assessed and responded to all the activity, tracking the room, participating, watching, conducting, occasionally redirecting a pitch or rhythm. She fixed a long scroll with the song lyrics to the wall and led the vocals in her throaty, rich contralto voice. At the beginning, Lamm played a theremin and, later, an accordion. Clusters of guitar and percussion players joined in at different times. A group of three singers arrived in the second hour and accompanied Lamm with rich harmonic voices. Occasionally, Lamm would make a request: more bass, more mic on the singers, less hiss. Recently, she told me, "I remember that I wrote one of the chords wrong, so we repeated one wrong chord all afternoon!" Meanwhile, the song was endless, reverberating in and out of refrains and melodies, shifting subtly to a more minor key or changing tempo. I was thankful Lamm arranged for a videographer, since my own camera effort was so distracted by the musical process. I think I remember a table of refreshments and hope I helped provide some sustenance for these musicians, who worked long and hard. By the third hour of the jam, I was mesmerized by the expression of joy that emanated from the gathering of twenty-odd people, utterly in keeping with the words of Kohan's song.

At the time of the jam session in 2010, Lamm wrote: "I think if I had seen her perform while she was alive, I would have thought it was corny. But looking through her journals I could really feel her spirit, a kind of prophetic voice that was trying to come through her. That's why I chose the song I did instead of her better-known "Fat Girl Blues," which I think would have been the more obvious choice. When she sang "Spirit Let Your Love Come Through," I could really feel it."

Kohan's archive box includes a colorful array of clothing—turquoise-and-orange patterned slip-on shoes, a bright pink t-shirt emblazoned with the words "All Fat Women Gathering," a gold sequined top, and a crisp white shirt with a large black musical staff appliqué. Under the clothing are photographs dating back to Kohan's childhood in Argentina, concert notices, music and lyrics, journals, scrapbooks, and correspondence. In a smaller box there are DVDs, audio recordings, and materials from her memorial. The collection form indicates that the materials were donated by Kohan's sister, Feliza Kohan.

Known for her big voice, flamboyant costumes, and showy stage presence, Kohan's best-known original song was "Fat Girl Blues." She died at fifty-five of congestive heart failure. Her obituary in the *Los Angles Times* stated:

> Born in 1948 in Argentina of Jewish descent, passed away on June 27, 2003 in Hollywood. Arriving in the U.S. in 1957 she learned English by singing show tunes. In the 60s she was with the L.A. All-City Choir and in 1965 toured with "Up With People." In 1971 she played for the Venice Free Theater. She was a regular at the Troubadour. She became active with feminist music and was a member of the L.A. Community Women's Chorus. George Winston produced her album "Finally Real" in 1984. She was often at Venice Beach singing Tangos with her Argentine compañeros.[33]

Lamm recently wrote: "My main memory of working with Silvia's archive was looking through all these little notebooks with lists and diary entries that felt so familiar and intimate. I remember finding a list of people to invite to a brunch, and my therapist was on the list. I remember a story about Silvia having a sexual experience in a hammock, where her takeaway was 'I love my friends.' It was so sweet and

wholesome and also so great to learn about her active sex life.
I really appreciated this glimpse into her world."

Nomy and Silvia were an ideal match because of the
centrality of music in both their lives, their Jewish identities, and their unapologetic and proud fat identities. Lamm
has described herself as a "bad ass, fat ass, Jew, dyke ampu-
tee." Her left foot was amputated at age three because of a
bone growth disorder, and she was fitted with a leg pros-
thesis. This trauma influenced Lamm's work about body
image. In my notes I found a list of people I called to the
GLBT Historical Society reading room for a meeting in
March 2010—eight new participants ready to meet their
archive matches. The memory lingers of sitting at a long
table with Lamm to my left. After leaving briefly, I returned
and visibly jumped at the sight of a disconnected leg on the
floor beside her chair. Embarrassed, I realized that Lamm,
for comfort, had taken off the prosthetic I didn't yet know
about. Lamm seemed nonplussed, clearly accustomed to
reactions like mine.

Ten years later, Lamm reflected:

When I see that I called Silvia corny ten years ago, I see
myself thinking everything that came before me wasn't as
cool. And now I see myself becoming a corny old queer
(May it be Her Will)! Silvia was a big, dramatic badass.
She was a Latina Jewish lesbian lounge singer who knew
how to put on a show, and while she wrote some of her
songs, most of her songs were covers, including the one I
based my project around. I didn't know until afterwards
that the song was actually written by Ferron and called
"Heart of Destruction."

I thought of Silvia as much older than me but realize
I am now probably older than she was when she was doing

a lot of her work. I am grateful to know Silvia as one of my queer ancestors and can feel the line extending back beyond her and then forward in time to the young queers making art now, and those to come.

If I could talk to Silvia today, I would want to connect with her around Jewish music and practice.

Luciano Chessa,
b. 1971

Larry DeCeasar,
1931–2002

"Prayer of an Aspiring Musician," aria and libretto,
performed by Don Tatro; 2009

Luciano Chessa is an experimental composer, musicologist,
and performance and visual installation artist from Sassari,
Italy. He recently moved to Berlin from San Francisco after
a two-year sojourn in New York—all places he travels to for
concerts and other opportunities. Chessa composes original
works, which he sometimes conducts or at other times plays
on a musical handsaw, piano, or Vietnamese dan bau, a
stringed instrument. I first met Chessa at the opening reception for a PLAySPACE Gallery group show in which
several of my *Quasi Lapis* gravestone photographs were on
display. Chessa was performing "Tom's Heart II" on his
musical saw. During the intermission, he and I bonded over
our mutual fascination with death and funerary memorials.
He later told me about the yearly summer solstice concert
"Garden of Memory" at the Oakland, California, Chapel of
the Chimes, where experimental musicians play in all the
nooks and crannies of that eccentric mausoleum. In one
room, designed to resemble a library, with large book forms
that contain cremains, I saw my second performance by
Chessa. Standing on a large crypt, an amp hooked up to his
bow, he raised his saw to the ceiling and played it like a vio-
lin, looking every bit like an ecstatic monk.

I matched Chessa to the archive labeled "The Papers and
Artifacts of Lawrence Filip DeCeasar a.k.a. Larry Langtry
(1931–2002)." Also known as Silver Dollar Larry and Larry
the Piano Man, DeCeasar was a flamboyant self-taught
musician who made his living playing honky-tonk piano
tunes in saloons and cocktail lounges from Louisiana to

Alaska. In Juneau during the early 1960s, he played at the Red Dog Saloon, where he became a disciple of Juneau Hattie Jessup, the Queen of Ragtime, who is pictured with him in several Polaroid snapshots. Even though Jessup was thirty years DeCeasar's senior, the two friends made a pact that whoever died first would come back to visit the other. According to an unattributed news clipping titled "The Piano Man," DeCeasar claimed she came back to visit six times after she died. "I didn't actually see her or hear her the way really psychic people do. I'm just a little bit psychic. But I've studied the occult and spiritualism for years. . . . I felt pressure, as if she was pushing against me. It was not at all uncomfortable." DeCeasar went on to say that he welcomed these visits. "Sometimes I miss Hattie very much. Strangely, my life has been a lot like hers. Neither of us had any close relatives for years. Our fathers died when we were very small. Neither of us ever learned to read music, we both played with gloves on, and we were crazy about people."

DeCeasar was active in San Francisco from the 1970s into the 1990s. He lived for many years at Maria Manor near San Francisco's Union Square, where he entertained informally with music and tales of his life as a self-trained piano player. DeCeasar's archive includes correspondence, personal and professional photographs, his astrological chart, appointment calendars, newspaper clippings, printed matter related to his memorial service, sheet music and set lists, and the glittering costumes he wore while performing. There are dozens of playlists written in green, blue, and red inks on cardboard scraps mixed in with several custom-sewn satin embroidered vests and cummerbunds, a pair of sequined gloves, elaborate cufflinks, and bejeweled bolero ties. Photo booth strips show DeCeasar in sequential self-conscious poses at different stages of his life. Faded color snapshots from performances show him at the piano, and, in one, curls of smoke from an ashtray sitting on the piano drift across the image. One photo reveals a tattoo inscribed right below a nipple: "Do not resuscitate in case of collapse." A printed sheet from his eulogy states that he was a dedicated spiritualist and metaphysician, and a printed card identifies him as a certified minister for the Church of the God Within.

At the bottom of this jumble of artifacts, Chessa spotted what was perhaps the least exotic item: a printed prayer card with the words of "Prayer of an Aspiring Musician." Chessa wrote, "All of a sudden, I was rapturously moved by a few clumsy, copyrighted devotional verses. Why? Larry was hardly an amateur. Was this a lesson in humility?" Chessa spoke this as a highly trained musician with a PhD. After his first encounter with the DeCeasar archive, he rushed home to compose an aria for voice and piano, which he imagined being sung in the soprano voice of male opera singer Don Tatro, someone he had worked with in the past.

Two months later Chessa and Tatro performed the aria in a concert series at the Old First Presbyterian Church in San Francisco. In a practice session, I joined the two of them with my video camera. Playing the score on the church piano, Chessa ended with a Fluxus-like performance in which he crumpled his paper score, adding this sound to the mix. Tatro sang the libretto based on DeCeasar's prayer card text, and I videotaped from start to finish. For the first *LINEAGE* exhibition, this video loops on a small screen with headphones. At the opening reception, Tatro sang Chessa's aria in his surprising, crystalline soprano voice.

Chessa wrote about his experience:

Our relationship is punctuated by a number of striking coincidences. Larry's box was filled with an odd collection of astrological charts, old photographs, sequined gloves, plastic jewelry, newspaper clippings, daily planners, pieces of folded paper with passages from the Gospel or important dates (Mario Lanza died 1959; Lillian Russell 1860–1922), red waistcoats, and an ordained-by-mail membership card issued from the Church of the God Within, Inc. At the bottom of Larry's file, in meticulously handwritten notebooks and on the backs of cardboard sheets, are Larry's playlists, which contain thousands of showtune titles, mostly pre-1928 tear-jerkers, all of which he could apparently play by heart on request. Larry's repertoire was incredible in all its flamboyant, memorized luxuriance.

Larry offered me a chance to experience a world I knew next to nothing about—the world of piano bars in post–World War II America. Our relationship is punctuated by a number of striking coincidences. In looking through his box, I found that he had performed several times at the Bucket of Blood Saloon in Virginia City, Nevada, a location I directly refer to in my piece "Quadri da una città fantasma" from 2003.

Soon after I formally introduced Chessa to DeCeasar's archive, Chessa emerged from the reading room at the GLBT Historical Society having just discovered the Bucket of Blood coincidence. Moved to tears, he wondered, "Was this simply a coincidence? Was it astrologically predetermined?" (I thought, Damn I'm a good matchmaker!) Though on a radically different career trajectory, Chessa connected very deeply to DeCeasar.

Twelve years after Chessa met Larry the Piano Man in the archives, he still thinks of him whenever feeling nostalgic for San Francisco, or whenever he reflects on his mortality or tries to work on a legal will. Chessa asks:

What remains of us queer once we are dead? More often than not we don't leave children. So, what will we leave?

A memory box with a few trinkets, some costume jewelry, plastic honors from dormant lodges, red-velvet gloves, toys, tear-jerkers, aspirations, hopes? And if so, to whom?

In Larry's box years ago, I had to face my future. I had to face my failures. It was Lacan-esque, it was Dickens-esque. If back then I feared what was coming, in growing up I realized that all that happens is always inevitable. I had been afraid I would grow up and be Larry. The thought of ending up alone alarmed me. While I wanted some distance from him, I could not help but notice how close we already were.

If anything, I get closer and closer to Larry with age. But with age something is changing in me. I am less alarmed. While I may not fear death, it's true that I do fear solitude and physical decay. So, I would love to ask Larry: Is it really that bad to grow older? I know I cannot say what he will answer. But what I wish Larry would say to me is, "Do realize that as long as the Muses visit us, and we visit them in the work of others, we won't truly be alone." As for what remains of us, the answer is ringing clearer and clearer to me: eventually nothing. So why worry?

Drawing by Chris E. Vargas

PART 3

Three Encounters
with Ghosts

Queer theorists are not alone in using the figure of the ghost as
a way to explain the apparitional social status of marginalized
subjects; indeed, the ghost is a powerful way of understanding
memory and identity.
—Molly McGarry, *Ghosts of Futures Past*

Part III showcases a recent extension of the *LINEAGE:
Matchmaking in the Archive* project. I wanted to incorporate
perspectives other than my own in considering the big issues
of queer lineage. I thought, Maybe my outlook is too paro-
chial and in need of expansion. Maybe if I invite writers well
known in queer circles, it will lend a patina of authority to
my book. Maybe it will expand my audience, be sexier, add
excitement.

And so, I invited three writers, who offer all of the above
to reflect on what queer lineage means to them. Jonathan D.
Katz, Michelle Tea, and Chris E. Vargas have their own

original ways of addressing ghosts and rendering queer lives visible. The eloquence of their thoughts and language contributes important perspectives to the work of engaging with our queer history.

Animating the Dead

BY JONATHAN D. KATZ

For many queers, coming out means encountering a past wholly different from one's own. At the point we claim our sexuality, some of us also choose to inherit a genealogy, arguably the sole genealogy that is heritable absent blood ties. And as we consider some of our ancestors, and their courage and persistence against odds and forces that dwarf what we confront today, it's natural to seek to measure ourselves against them, wondering how they did what they did, knowing in advance that, more likely than not, we will be found wanting. Here the archive can resemble a vast, albeit spectator-less, private coliseum where we test ourselves against our precursors, wondering if we'd survive as well as they did, if we'd have their courage, if we could possibly live through, as so many of them did, conditions of unimaginable, crushing constraint. They took risks we can't imagine, suffered unthinkable indignities, dared far more than we ever could. No wonder "It gets better" has become our permanent generational mantra, for we know how comparatively soft we are. To survive what they survived is one thing, but they then bedazzled it with humor, sass, and wit, defanging the hellishness and in the process not only remaking their world but seeding ours. Like it or not, we are connected to them, these ancestors we've never met with whom we have no real connection save an imagined one. But intimacy is always far more conceptual than physical, and in the archive we can find a real form of it. Matchmaking is a dialogue between people, and except in the most obvious ways, it doesn't matter if one of them is dead.

Dead or not, the ones in the archive are the winners. The losers are the interminable generations of those who dissimulated, to others or themselves, about who they really were, what they wanted and needed. They lived faceless lives of quiet desperation, or loneliness, or both. Some made other innocent people miserable by proving unable to give these blameless ones—their own husbands, wives, and even children—the kind of love that was withheld from them. Yet more painful still, there were those who never knew love at all, who felt they couldn't be loved because of who they were, who could never understand what so many poems or lyrics really meant because their emotional bandwidth was so restricted. Whether out of fear or obliviousness, they closed themselves off from our most human feelings because of a culture that despised them and caused them to despise themselves. Perhaps unique among the reviled and shunned, many of them stripped their own humanity away before it could be done to them. Stunted and shamed, they lived in a shadow world where they made lives without human warmth and the prospect of communion. To think of the generations across the centuries who lived and died not knowing the simple emotions we take for granted, who shuffled on and off this earth, with the sole aim of trying only to kill what they could have offered others and been offered in return.

So we queers commune with the dead, and for a host of different reasons: as an act of respect for those who bucked the rules and made a space for themselves heedless of the costs, which in turn helped make a space for us; as an act of reparation for those who couldn't be, and so we now speak their queer names as if it will heal something torn in the world; as a gesture of gratitude that measures how far we've come; as an act of love for those who died unloved; as an exercise in power and authority, reshaping the world we inherited by giving voice to long silent voices that can challenge all the mystifications, stubborn pieties, and deliberate erasures that have kept us down. And that doesn't even count the main rationale, to rebuild our community in the face of those who worked, and continue to work, so hard to destroy it. Our enemies in the law, in the church, in medicine, and in public life realized early on that the best way to keep us down was to segregate us from one another, transforming the shared ground of collective action into an individual instance of pathology. Without one another, we were vastly easier to control and suppress. Isolation was our prison. So now we conjure a vast missing army as we go forward, knitting together what was torn asunder. There is safety in numbers.

It's not hard to fall in love with the dead, not least because they are a ready, uncomplaining, and largely blank screen on which to project all our own joys and needs and obsessions. In fact, while we claim to be listening to them, in point of fact, it's the dead who echo us. Ceaselessly, they are animated and reanimated by our interests, seemingly revived by our attentions. Despite our many differences, they are never annoying, for they take our side in every argument. So malleable and patient and kind, it's almost as if we dreamed them up.

Straight culture uses the term *marriage* to describe a twelfth-century, sixteenth-century, nineteenth-century, and twentieth-century compact between two people of different genders, despite the fact that each of these manifested such vastly different social, economic, religious, and spiritual meanings that, to all intents and purposes, they have next to nothing in common. The idea that love animated a medieval marriage would have been as embarrassingly laughable as the notion that a seamless transfer of capital describes our own. But because heterosexuality has long owned the stage of history, we have no trouble with using this manifestly shifty, inadequate, even empty term to describe this series of mutating social meanings. What the term *marriage* is to straight culture, *LGBTQ* is to queers. We often have really no idea what sexual differences meant in the past on a social or psychic basis, and what we think we have in common with the dead is frankly almost always up for grabs. But the reason straights use the single term *marriage* to describe a ritual unfolding over centuries in a huge array of contexts is to allow for historical continuity, for to be a culture, you need to have a history. In the archive, we claim that history, annexing the lives of those we find there and recruiting them to our very contemporary political cause of building that history long denied us, enforcing a collectivity in the face of repeated attempts to isolate, denying us the company of our forebearers. History may be about the past, but it's for the living and answers only to them.

The chronicle of papers burned, love letters destroyed, photographs and documents incinerated is long and painful. Even in my own lifetime, I witnessed the families of men who died in the AIDS plague actively destroy the truth of their own relatives' lives at a point when they could no longer object, forcing them back into the closet and into their own blinkered mid-twentieth-century narratives of family respectability. They compelled surviving partners to sit well behind the family at memorial services, ignored and unacknowledged, while the blood relations of those they disowned and despised plundered the spoils of the couple's collective existence that, because it didn't exist in the eyes of the law, didn't exist. One friend salvaged a single photograph from a decade-plus relationship, watching the family that hated them treat their joint property like a tag sale where everything was free. We have weathered such acts of violence after acts of violence, a centuries-long chronicle of forced erasures, deliberate deceit and duplicity. And evidence of queer lives, even when it heroically survives its planned destruction, can, and often is, dismissed. Such dismissals can be as simple as "you're projecting" since the default position in history was, and remains, the "straightening up" of untidy historical narratives.

On the rare occasions when the evidence is either too voluminous or compelling to sweep under the carpet, the same homophobic discomfort is often gussied up as an impartial scholarly demand that we prove the exact meaning of the terms for sexual difference in the period in question—this often by scholars who have no trouble describing "marriage" in past centuries without any qualification. Of course, in the face of centuries of violent obliteration and the historical oblivion that was its goal, the comparatively few artifacts that remain are cherished. They are perforce largely modern, so when it comes to earlier periods, we give ourselves greater latitude to speculate, to paper over the gaps, infill the silences, and justify our creative recuperation as a measured, even just, response to the wave after wave of violence that has deliberately worked to destroy our history.

But as much as I'd like to claim the right of wholesale invention, in truth we don't, at least not out of whole cloth. Instead, we sense something that eludes the normative standards of evidence, we catch a whiff of something familiar, resonant. When you're queer, the dead speak to you in a shared language, and we do our best to translate that language for those who lack our fluency. It's often a language of feints and baffles, as eloquent in its patterns of omission as for what it affirms, a palimpsest of gendered pronouns, photos, and letters judiciously edited and cut. We queers can still read these tea leaves, and once we pick up a scent, we can be relentless in following it through. It's hardly an invention to shade and recolor the gray lives that result when everything lively and true has been wiped away.

The archive, like the past itself, doesn't exist to sit passively in boxes; it's not there to be found, it's there to be used. Doing research in archives is like writing a sentence with only nouns; to have it make sense, you have to supply the verbs. It's axiomatic that the verbs you supply are the ones you care about, the ones you like to use. And someday someone else will come along with their choice of verbs and potentially challenge your choice and that's all to the good. The goal isn't to tell the story, for that presumes that the story and we are somehow separated, cleaved. Instead, in doing history we tell our own contemporary story, placing the facts of the past in the order we need. In the same way that utopias are really the most revealing analysis of the ills of the present moment, archival histories are pictures of what we value now. When, in the future, others will analyze our archival histories, they will learn more about us than the people we claim to write about.

LINEAGE: Matchmaking in the Archive, in its pairing of historical and contemporary figures, knows that desire is the electric current that fuels the often dusty and tedious work of archival research. When spelunking in the dark, it's the only power source we have. But we know well, especially thanks to the recent "#MeToo" movement, how easily desire can overwrite another's will, appropriating them to narratives not of their own making, making them do things that in life they might have found untoward or ill conceived. When we make the archive speak, we engage in an act of ventriloquism, necessarily making our subjects over into our hand puppets. While they don't object, consent remains a basic courtesy when making another's lips move to the rhythms of our speech. And we will never, and can never, earn their consent. And so, we must admit that digging in the archives is never really about them, it's always about us. (We queers don't recruit in the present, but we most certainly do so in the past.) But, and this is critical, we don't ask the dead to say things that we want them to say. Instead, we try to listen to them, and merely turn up the volume on the voices we think we hear. Broadcasting the faint whispers in the archive is an act of homage, of respect, and most centrally of thanks. We owe them, quite literally, our lives.

Magical Thinking

BY MICHELLE TEA

A witch once told me that I have no ancestors looking out for me. None. Zero. Zilch. Those great-great-great-grandpeople who've gone before me, those eighteenth cousins twice removed, those aunts and uncles whose DNA twists hardily through my body, nowhere to be found. They are not draped ethereally around me, like a posse of gossamer bodyguards, protecting me from the evil eye and opening roads to success via whatever obstacle-busting methods the dead are granted in the otherworld. No long-dead French woman I'd like to think passed on a gene for style and melodrama is silently guiding my hand as I reach to pluck earrings from my jewelry box (nor is she shuffling me toward a designer thrift score tucked on a rack at Goodwill). The Irish ancestors who left me with a tendency toward superstition and an undeniable gift of gab are not sending me omens and portents in the form of bird feathers or freaky dreams or a clock that seems to always flash 11:11. The Polish folks who bequeathed to me a certain melancholy, a yearning for revolution, and, I think, alcoholism have not been a psychic support system during these seventeen years of sobriety. When it comes to dead-ancestor and living-lineage relationships, I am an orphan.

As a person prone to magical thinking, this info was a deep letdown. Maybe it is a consequence of being raised Catholic, being stuffed in a plaid uniform and sent to Catholic school until the tarantula tangles of my goth hairdo finally got me kicked out in ninth grade, but I have always felt—or wanted to feel—an otherworldly presence keeping me company in this life. Being raised to think that a Santa-esque God was constantly keeping an eye on me, mildly punishing, sure, but overall benevolent and protective, kept my body alert to signs of that sixth sense, an electrical intuition that was most likely connected to some channel higher than myself. God, I thought as a kid, or maybe one of the cool, tortured saints I was fascinated with—Bernadette, whose own sixth sense had revealed to her the presence of the Virgin Mary as she prayed in a grotto, whatever that was. Religion class at Our Lady of Assumption School was filled with tales of miracles: angels visiting young women to hip them to the miracle seed sprouting in their womb; Party Jesus fermenting some water into wine and conjuring other snacks to keep the peckish revelers happy. The Devil, also a magic spirit, shape-shifting into a fruit-pushing snake. So many saints, serenely holding platters of whatever body parts were wrenched from their bodies—Agatha with her little cakes of breast, Lucy and the balls of her eyes. In this way, I was raised in a magical world, a world that promised the return of this chimera, Jesus, part man part god part son part dad. I figured the Second Coming would need another perfect vessel, like the one found in Virgin Mary back in the days of the Bible. Mary, the chosen one, visited by a freaking angel, descending from the sky on muscular wings, probably a golden horn or a flag of some sort in his hand, perhaps a gleaming sword; angels seemed to have a lot of props. Imagine, to be so special one of God's own angels sought you out, chose the meat of your body to build us all a messiah. In second grade, I knew it was me. Then I got a bad mark on a test.

There is this sensation I have when playing bingo—stay with me—when a string of numbers gets called, and I don't have them, and I just know the odds, considering all the elderly that surround me, frantically daubing their pages, haloed with cigarette smoke, their cluster of lucky things arranged before their cards, a little bingo hall altar with coins and rabbits' feet and troll dolls and snapshots of their dearly departed or lucky grandkids. Odds are, some of these players marked those numbers on their own cards, and the game is over for me. I keep playing, of course; anything can happen in bingo, and as bad as my eyes are they've got to be better than those of some of these octogenarians who didn't clock that I16 or N33. Maybe I can win due to someone else's mistake. But probably I won't. Soon enough, "Bingo!" is cawed out of someone's happy mouth and the hall rasps with the sound of a hundred pages of bingo being ripped from the game, balled up and flung into the trash bags taped to the end of the cluttered tables. And, "Shit." Lots of "Shit," hissed from the mouths of grandmas.

Getting the bad mark on the test I guess I'd planned to do well on was sort of like that. Maybe I had been in the running to be the next Virgin Mary—I was good enough, felt magic enough—but certainly, odds were that some other little girls in the running had aced their tests, and I could feel myself dropped out of the race. My eyes stung. I took the test and slid it up underneath my navy blue cardigan, the paper crackling against the length of my torso. I raised my hand and asked Ms. Poire if I could go to the bathroom. The girls' room was down a flight of stairs, a long, cold basement room painted blue. The gleaming trash can stood at the entrance. I pulled my test from my sweater and ripped it up so that if the janitor, Mr. Andrekis, found it, he wouldn't know which child had disposed of their test in such a shady way. I went back upstairs. I didn't know who I thought I was fooling. God was the only judge of the World's Next Top Virgin Mother, and he saw everything, so he knew I flunked out and was watching me right then as I tearfully trashed the test. But how to parse out magical thinking from a curriculum of magical thinking?

I'm telling you this because I was raised to be a witch. What is Catholicism if not witchcraft? Even the other Christians know this and disdain the baroque or rococo aesthetics of the church, with its red velvet everything and haze of frankincense and hoarder's gallery of statuary, its flagrantly pagan leftovers, the blood drinking, the rose windows, the presence of an actual Goddess. The other Christians are practicing their own witchcraft too, to be sure, but it's so normcore and boring, except those wild snake handlers and tongue speakers. I was raised to believe that someone was watching me always, on hand to help, and I didn't mind. I liked thinking of a world just beyond this one, up in the clouds or swirling unseen right in front of our faces. Ghosts. Aliens swooping down in crafts high-tech with invisibility. Bigfoot living at the edge of the forest, peeping at campers. When I became goth it was vampires; what if they were real, was I worthy? I was a virgin until I was eighteen, not for any particular reason (aside from most of my boyfriends being fake bisexual gay boys), and it was a comfort to know that it kept me more attractive to those creatures of the night. I binged Anne Rice and imagined being watched by a slender, pale-faced creature, hair slick and black and inking into his face, his clothing *literally* from the nineteenth century. I was the girl of his dreams. Me, in my Salvation Army black clothes, my face sticky white with actual clown makeup and a dusting of baby powder. In the other room, my family ate Top Ramen in front of the television blaring

Growing Pains and *Cheers*. They called me *antisocial* because I wouldn't come out and bathe in the secondhand smoke with them. I stayed in my room, the linoleum floor of which I vandalized with black nail polish, Halloween decorations dangling year-round from the blinds, blinds kept open so that my fantasy vampire could see me clearly from where he perhaps perched in a tree, in his bat formation.

So, my witch had told me that maybe my grandmother didn't like that I was queer. My witch was herself queer, had recently designed an oracle deck featuring a card titled "Leather," in which bare-assed men leaned against a bar, their cheeks doming out from the seams of their chaps. Another was "Cock," and the package that pushed against the watercolor-blue denim was most definitely man-made. "Slutty" was a femme dressed in the iconic femme uniform of full slip and fishnets, set against a chain-link fence. "Pussy" was an au natural frizz, "Cheap Fuck" a tangle of limbs. I knew my witch was being straight with me, so to speak, when she told me my dead grandmother wasn't psyched at my life choices. It was disappointing to hear, mostly because the earthly plane is so swamped with ignorance, I had conjured a belief that the hereafter granted everyone access to a higher consciousness, one more like mine. My grandmother hadn't seemed like the worst homophobe; I still remember her glee after returning from a day trip to Boston to see *Mommie Dearest* with my gay cousin Brian, closeted, sure, but he was a hairdresser, and, well, gay, and wasn't really fooling anybody. But I guess people are weird about their own kids and grandkids.

The knowledge that my ancestors had abandoned me was with me as I stood at my altar, generally the top shelf of a smaller bookcase, arranged with items that represent the elements: Crystals for rocks, or sometimes earth dug from my yard. Found feathers for air, plus something to burn, for the smoke. Candles for fire, seashells and a little cup of water for water. The cup is *very* little, in fact, a yellow glass mug fit for a doll that was once part of a miniature decorative punch bowl belonging to my grandmother, who was mad at me. I gazed at it on the shelf, a plastic mermaid from some party soaking in it. If I wasn't sending all this energy out to my ancestors, if it wasn't they I was asking to intervene in my destiny, open roads and whatnot, bring me hot lovers, help me to stop obsessing over those who have ceased to love me, who was I in conversation with? It seemed important to know. At the very least, magic requires focus, and I needed someone or something to focus on.

And so, I called on my queer ancestors. It's sort of a no-brainer, and it happened easily enough. A black-and-white photo of Marsha P. Johnson ripped from a magazine, that iconic one of her holding a cigarette and a sign reading "Power to the People." I don't even think I understood who she was, just that I loved her, and she was clearly magic, and so she went on my altar. And so, I began to offer my devotions. The urge to be devotional is as strong as any other thing I want for, and here was a person a devotion sprang instinctively toward. I felt it in my heart chakra, a grateful rotation. A kinship, a humble recognition. And so, I began to call out to my queer ancestors, of whom there are certainly thousands. All the unseen unknown nameless queers who came before and possibly, hopefully watch me in my life and are happy for me, maybe they live alongside me, vicariously, happy for my freedoms, not like bitter still-living elders wanting to punish the youngsters for not knowing how bad they have it, resentful at their actually having made things better. I didn't get that vibe at all from this ancestor I now know to be Mx. Johnson. Calling out to my queer chosen dead family made me wonder what other chosen ancestors I might claim, and I called out to my sex work ancestors. Even though I have not held that occupation in decades, it marked me deeply and set me on my path, and I feel that devotional kinship at the thought of them. My feminist ancestors. My literary ancestors. I call out to them in a vague way, just letting any such spirits that might be lingering about know that they are welcome at my altar, that I love them for the lives they lived and the risks they took to build them, for the pleasure they sought, for the way they lived beyond the codes of their times. These days I call out to white abolitionist ancestors, ask them to guide my thoughts and actions. Because we are the next iteration. I think that is part of the allure of this connection. The imagining that my life might have a continual purpose that is larger than hustling rent or making sure my kid does his homework or cleaning the trash can so whatever foul-smelling slop festering at the bottom doesn't kill us all. That those things that occupy so much of the precious time of this, my singular life (for even if I have a life again, it certainly will not be this one) is nothing, that there is a larger game I'm playing, necessarily hidden from me. I like this lineage and I like this devotion and I call out to the queer hooker misfit writers who help me find my existential place. Thank for you your life, for having lived. The choices you made impact the choices I make in thousands of ways I will never comprehend. *This* is magic. It is beyond blood. It is my place in the queer cosmos.

Mi Transtepasado / My Trancestor: Amelio Robles Ávila

BY CHRIS E. VARGAS

Trans people want to understand that we are not alone. We want to know that other people, across time and place, have been identifying and living their lives beyond the expectations related to the genders assigned to them at birth. We do this by forging bonds to ancestors from the archive, recruiting them as mentors, or even guardian angels. But because gender expectations shift over time and differ culturally, I know when I look to my trancestors the identification is not always a perfect fit. And that's OK.

It's not that my family archive isn't interesting, but there's no one life or experience among my blood relatives with which I can fully identify. I am of mixed ethnicity. I grew up in the San Fernando Valley in Southern California. My mom is a West Virginia–born, California-raised white girl. My dad is Mexican American and grew up in Los Angeles, but his parents are from Mexico. My mom and dad divorced before I was a year old, and while they were both in my life when I was growing up, I am closer to my mom's side of the family. I had a personal relationship neither to the "back east" of my white grandparents nor to Mexico. Aside from California itself, of course, which was Mexico until a short time ago—until the 1848 Treaty of Guadalupe Hidalgo to be exact—and demographically and culturally still very much is.

I don't remember how I stumbled upon the biography of Amelio Robles Ávila, the famous *coronel* of the Mexican Revolution, born in 1889 in Xochipala, in the Mexican state of Guerrero. Perhaps it was from the various trans history blogs I follow or the excellent trans history podcast *One from the Vaults*, made by London-based, Canadian-born Morgan M. Page. One of these led me to the articles and scholarship of the Mexico City–based academic Gabriela Cano, who has done invaluable research and to whom I owe a huge debt for all that I know about this important figure.

Robles is a masculine military figure, full of grit and machismo, a straight man and not necessarily someone with whom I would identify in the present. My own gender is pretty gay, and as a U.S.-born person of mixed ethnicity with only one root of my family tree in Mexico, I share the common experience among many U.S.-born Latinx people of never feeling Latinx "enough." I don't doubt that this is a result of colonialism, but I can't articulate exactly why. I am also not patriotic and have never understood the urge to risk life and limb for my country, especially a country that doesn't look favorably on people like myself. While I believe everyone should be treated with dignity, the struggle for trans inclusion in the military was never mine. But Robles is trans and Mexican, and because I've spent so much time digging around in a disproportionately white trans history, he piqued my curiosity.

I am the founder and executive director of the Museum of Transgender Hirstory & Art (MOTHA), a conceptual museum I dreamed up in 2013. I launched the project because at that time trans art and culture were beginning to get noticed, and I wanted to use the project to think critically about what is gained and lost when a historically marginalized identity is absorbed into the mainstream, specifically museums, academia, and the mass media. When trans narratives, or any historically marginalized peoples' narratives, are delivered to a mass audience beyond themselves, biographical nuances fall away at best or are misrepresented and violently disrespected at worst.

Trans people are more likely to experience discrimination in health care, employment, and housing than cisgender people are, and a precarious life isn't conducive to the preservation of artifacts. This means that the more affluent and, more often than not, whiter of my trans siblings are overrepresented in most archives. Robles is no different. He is actually remembered in his hometown as "La Güera," or the fair-skinned blonde girl. As Walter Benjamin famously put it, in a quotation sometimes attributed to Winston Churchill, "History is written by the victors." This particular transcestor was victorious during his life, though he lost control of his narrative in death. But I'm getting ahead of myself.

Robles was born in November 1889 in the pueblo Xochipala in the state of Guerrero, located in the southwestern part of Mexico, a few hours to Acapulco going south and Mexico City to the north. Robles came from a middle-class family. His father, who owned land and a small mescal factory, died when he was young. One of six siblings, Robles learned to ride and tame horses and to shoot guns as a child—activities generally associated with a masculine gender.

In his early twenties, he took part in the Mexican Revolution, a decadelong struggle from 1910 to 1920 to wrest power from the oligarchical Porfirio Díaz. From the revolution emerged the modern Mexican democratic state and the 1917 Mexican Constitution, which is still in use today. During the first part of the Mexican revolutionary war, Robles joined the Maderistas, and then he fought with the Zapatistas for five or six years until 1918. After that, he joined forces with Álvaro Obregón, who later became president of Mexico.

In 1913, at the age of twenty-three, not too long after joining the revolutionary forces, Robles started dressing and living as a man. He never had surgery or took hormones, he simply dressed in a way that downplayed any feminine aspects of his body. The scholar Cano mentions his choice of men's shirts with big pockets to disguise any semblance of a female-bodied chest. According to local lore, he was also known to shoot his pistol with his left hand while holding a cigar in the right, perfectly illustrated by a studio photograph of him leaning on a chair with a cigar in one hand and holding open his coat to reveal a pistol holster on his hip with the other.

In order to secure his male legitimacy, and thus military credentials, Robles forged his birth certificate. The new birth certificate he had made contained the same information as his original but with a masculinization of his given name, Amelio Malaquías Robles Ávila. All other details, such as his father's and mother's names, his date and place of birth, remained the same.

I transitioned at twenty-seven and I, too, left home to do so. I transferred from Los Angeles Community College to finish my undergraduate degree at the University of California, Santa Cruz. I used my proximity to San Francisco to take advantage of the free and trans-competent health care there, but because I lived in Santa Cruz, this required me to forge some documents. A friend had told me about a free trans youth clinic, but I was two years too old to qualify. That didn't stop me. I probably could've accessed trans health care with my student insurance, but there was no guarantee the doctor would "get it," so it was worth it to me to assume a different residence and age on paper. I should've used an address where I actually lived, because eventually my unpaid bills caught up to me, and I had to forge a different document to get out of that jam. Not so long ago, at my current job I engaged in more creative trickery on my hiring paperwork, specifically my childhood immunization records. I did this to avoid drawing attention to the fact that I was not born male, since I had all my current records changed to "male"—except my birth certificate. Unlike Robles I've never needed to produce my assigned-female-at-birth certificate, so I've never bothered to change it. Also, I feel conflicted about erasing that part of my past, even if it is purely administrative.

Robles was a decorated veteran and very well recognized for his military service. In 1948, he obtained a medical certificate that would allow him to be admitted to the Confederation of Veterans of the Revolution. In order to do so, Robles was subjected to a medical exam confirming his age and health and scars from six gunshot wounds. Who knows how it all went down, but the exam was done in such a way as not to betray his biological sex. In 1970, the Mexican secretary of defense recognized Robles as a veteran of the revolution. In 1974, the Secretaría de la Defensa Nacional recognized him as an official *veterano* of the revolution, using the masculine grammatical gender.

For the majority of his life, from his early twenties on, he lived and identified as a man. In December 1984, he died at the age of ninety-five. According to his neighbors, he'd threaten anyone who'd refer to him in the feminine. One neighbor said: "I never called him ma'am, I always said Mr. Robles, because he would take out his pistol to whoever called him woman or lady." Even in his own family, his younger relatives would address him as *tío* or *abuelo*, uncle or grandfather, and only learned of his unique gender identity when they were older. Cano writes that he embodied such a *machista*, or misogynist, and toxic masculinity that, later in life, neighbors and friends described him as a drunk womanizer with a dirty mouth, who likely killed more than one person in violent interpersonal conflicts.

After his death, things get tricky.

All through his life he lived as male and demanded to be addressed as such. His military positions affirmed a masculine gender in the battlefield, where his bravery and valiance were sought after and valued. But upon his death, the way he is memorialized gets caught up in the writing of a nationalist narrative, specifically a feminist one that seeks to celebrate women's involvement in the revolution. This is seen in the highlighting of the important contributions made by *soldaderas*. *Soldaderas* were women who actively participated in the Mexican Revolution in ranking military positions or as combatants, nurses, or simply "camp followers," women who offered services and companionship to the military men and who sometimes dressed in a more masculine way. They donned masculine dress to be taken more seriously as ranking officers or to desexualize themselves to fend off unwanted advances from other soldiers. Many accounts of *soldaderas* emphasize their resuming straight, feminine, domestic lives after the war.

The popular image of "La Adelita" is synonymous with the image of the *soldadera*. The diminutive of the woman's name Adela, La Adelita is an image of a feminine, patriotic archetype of the revolution. She is perhaps based on Adela Velarde Pérez, a young nurse who served in the revolution. But her legacy grows and endures, and La Adelita is remembered in various aspects of pop culture. She appears in songs like the famous revolutionary-era *corrido*, a narrative song genre popular from Mexican independence to the revolution. Her likeness also appears in popular images like the one hanging over my desk on a kitschy tear-away month calendar I got from the popular New Mexico spot Cafe

Pasqual's in Santa Fe. In this image, La Adelita sits side-saddle on a rearing golden horse; she is fair-skinned, with golden brown braids emerging from her sombrero and cascading down her embroidered huipil-style blouse. She waves a red flag of victory overhead as male soldiers do the same in the background.

Robles's image, of course, does not fit this idealized feminized image of La Adelita or *las soldaderas*. If I were to insert myself into an image of Mexican Revolution, it would be somewhere between Amelio Robles Ávila and La Adelita, maybe if his suit had some embroidered flourishes, and if these figures weren't so associated with combat and war. I value the historical role of revolutionary uprisings in history, but honestly, I'm not that brave. I'd offer to design the revolutionary broadsheet and posters.

Robles's legacy endures in his hometown in contradictory ways. A primary school, Escuela Primaria Urbana Federal "Coronel Robles," established in 1966, bears his name in recognition of his donation of the school grounds to the community. Another institution in town is a community and local history museum, Casa Museo Coronela Amelia "La Güera" Robles, which contains furniture and personal items from the *coronel*. The nickname that appears on the museum signage, "La Güera," misgenders Robles and references him as fair and thus, according to normative white Western beauty standards, more desirable and more beautiful. To drive another nail in the proverbial, and in this case literal, misgendering coffin, his tombstone in the local cemetery reads "Aquí yacen los restos de la coronela zapatista." "Here lie the remains of the Zapatista *coronela*." Not *coronel*.

There is an unsubstantiated rumor that at the end of Robles's life he requested burial as a woman, perhaps to make right with a Catholic God. I can't help but draw the association with the problematic trans cult classic *Let Me Die a*

Woman (1978), but in this case the gender is distorted—in the movie, trans women want to die as WOMEN, not their assigned male sex. But maybe this rumor was deployed to uphold Robles's image as a feminine revolutionary war hero. Maybe people wanted to believe he regretted his gender choices. Or maybe people never respected his gender self-determination in life, and it carried over in death. Or maybe we all just remember what we want and ignore the rest.

Forging archival bonds is always lopsided. It goes just one way. I feel slightly conflicted about my absorption of Robles's biography into a transgender history. Amelio Robles Ávila never called himself trans. Just as the development of a feminist national narrative uses Robles in self-serving ways, so do I. I'm seeking to absorb him into a trans history that he may or may not have wanted to be included in. But since we're always remembering and memorializing from our own biased temporality, historical identification will always be a self-serving project. And I'm OK with that.

More than identification, what I am seeking in Robles is a connection to the ancestral homeland of my dad's family, the Mexico that was so close to where I grew up in Southern California but which I never fully knew. I don't align with or condone Robles's (or anyone's) straight toxic masculinity, and this among many differences between us also makes our connection an imperfect fit. But I'm not one to shy away from problematic role models. As an artist, I am experienced not only in taking what I like and leaving the rest but also in taking liberties—liberties to re-imagine difficult aspects of people's lives in order to build role models that better suit me. I know that searching for transcestors in the archive is self-seeking in more than one sense. I am seeking aspects of myself in history and it's selfish. It's something we all do. At least I'm up front about it.

Sources

Cano, Gabriela. "Gender and Transgender in the Mexican Revolution: The Shifting Memory of Amelio Robles." In *Women Warriors and National Heroes: Global Histories*, edited by Boyd Cothran, Joan Judge, and Adrian Shubert, 179–196. London: Bloomsbury Academic, 2020.

———. "Revolution." *TSQ: Transgender Studies Quarterly* 1, no. 1–2 (2014): 178–180.

———. "Unconcealable Realities of Desire: Amelio Robles's (Transgender) Masculinity in the Mexican Revolution." In *Sex in Revolution: Gender, Politics, and Power in Modern Mexico*, edited by Jocelyn Olcott, Mary Kay Vaughan, and Gabriela Cano, 35–56. Durham, NC: Duke University Press, 2007.

———. "Inocultables realidades del deseo Amelio Robles, masculinidad (transgénero) en la Revolución." In *Género, Poder y Política en el México Posrevolucionario*, edited by Jocelyn Olcott, Mary Kay Vaughan, and Gabriela Cano, 71. México, FCE/UAM–Iztapalapa, 2009.

Page, Morgan M. "Revolutionary Man!" *One from the Vaults*, Patreon, February 14, 2018. https://www.patreon.com/posts/oftv-bonus-ep-8-16997677.

West Coast Celebration II
and Conference of
Old Lesbians

August 4 - 6, 1989
Seven Hills Conference Center
San Francisco State University
800 Font St.
San Francisco, CA

Adrienne Fuzee
2003-27
#19.7
Box 3

NO
PARKING
7AM-6PM
SUNDAYS
HOLIDAYS
EXCEPTED

Protest!
THE SLAUGHTER
OF Spain's
UNDERGROUND
FIGHTERS

HELP
MAKE MA
TOMB

PART 4

Lineages of Desire

Someone will remember us / I say / even in another time.
—Sappho, translation by Anne Carson

Sappho's lyric promises memory across death: once we and
everyone we know and everyone who knows us is dead, someone
is still going to think about us. We will be in history.... It is what
Christopher Nealon refers to in *Foundlings* as the "message in
- the bottle" dispatched from the queer past—sent seeking a
"particular historical kind of afterlife."
—Heather Love, *Feeling Backward: Loss and the Politics
of Queer History*

LINEAGE: Matchmaking in the Archive expanded my
social world in indelible ways. Over a period of seven years,
I perused over ninety-seven archives representing individual
lives, as my notebooks now remind me. I matched twenty-
four living individuals to an archive; nineteen participants
pursued the collaboration to create a piece that was exhibited, read, or performed. As the *LINEAGE* project unfolded,
new people approached me asking to be matched; each time

I would return to my old cruising ground, the aisles filled with potential candidates. The arrangement of boxes had inevitably shifted: people die, new collections arrive at the GLBT Historical Society, new kids on the block waiting for their spot on a shelf. There were times when I had the sense of having launched a cottage industry, one that I needed to expand beyond myself as sole proprietor and think about successors.

The question I kept asking was, How do we know a person after they die? I wondered what it meant to enter into a relationship with someone who is dead, and why people were eager to do so. As matchmaker, I became aware of my own historical promiscuity; but how did that work for the nineteen participants in their one-on-one relationships with the other side? Do we still need a nonnormative and destabilized approach to intimacy, something outside our normal queer lives and loves? Molly McGarry, in writing about the relationship of writers like Radclyffe Hall and Walt Whitman to Spiritualism, states in *Ghosts of Futures Past*, "These subjects made sense of their own queer time through spiritual theories of embodiment that offered forms of meaning that secular science refused " and, later, "Temporality functions here as the difference most difficult to bridge, the ultimate otherness."[1] McGarry uses the figure of the ghost as a way to understand the apparitional social status of marginalized subjects. This history is seen as a kind of haunting that comes back and informs the present. The specter of becoming familiar with ghosts opens us up to possession, an enchanted and sometimes erotic state. The process of opening an archive box, of absorbing what is inside and what you imagine beyond its confines, brings back a person's life queerly. A neat linear sequence of time becomes disordered as you relate to the person at all stages of their life. Like any romance, this process is marked by mystery, by the lure of the unknown, and by secrets—all the raw ingredients of fantasy.

But what exactly can these objects and documents, which have outlived a person, tell us? It seems that giving participants one archive to focus on, one person's life, had a unique power. I wonder if this is our most accessible way into history—not through grand narratives or identity politics, but through a simple one-to-one connection that we partially read and partially imagine. As matchmaker, I found that there was plenty to get off on. In the tradition of older women who engage in this service, I researched different traditions of matchmaking and set about learning how to do it. In the end, simple hunches, demographics, and knowledge about shared interests steered my process. Sometimes I let an archive point me to a person; other times talking with a person pointed me to a particular archive. I learned how to launch relationships and invented the means to witness every detail of how they evolved. The dialogue, images, objects, music, and writing that emerged from these uncommon connections became my markers of success. It was a kind of archive midwifery, a highly voyeuristic, undoubtedly manipulative, and totally magical experience.

In the process of writing this book, I asked the nineteen participants about their current thoughts on their archive match and the work they created a decade ago. It seems only fair that I ask myself these questions too. Which archives linger with me now, and what has changed? What seduced me, what touched me beyond my role in matchmaking? It might be that I owe the dead for spying on them. In some cases, the three-way connection between me, an archive, and a participant grew complicated, raising thorny questions that demanded discussion. Just as with all nineteen participants, my connection to the archives of the dead touched my life, touched me, in profound and very personal ways.

In writing this book, my autobiographical connections have intensified. The time represented within an archive box is rarely linear or orderly—a person's letters, photos, and objects often meander spatially between baby shoes and funeral notices with no tidy boundaries. It strikes me that this is not unlike how memory works as it zigzags across time, coming to consciousness in unexpected sequences. It is not unlike my own disorderly collection of stuff from across the decades of my life, my untended archive that lurks in the recesses of my home and my memory.

I am now close in age to many of the archived people whose lives I explored. Others were born after me, and their life-spans seem sadly attenuated in comparison. When I look at the gender-ambiguous lesbians pictured in Guy Duca's archive, lesbians who were adults before I reached puberty, I feel an odd nostalgia for a period before my time, one in which I conjure queer underground families. In this romantic fantasy, these images help ameliorate the general paucity of lesbian representation in older gay archives. I imagine I would have liked Duca. He was born eleven years before me, but his life is frozen at an age that now seems young, fifty-three. I have outlived him by several decades.

A Match of My Own

There is an archive I haven't yet mentioned. At some point in my matchmaking, I grew lonely. I wanted a match for myself, someone whose archive I could let inspire a piece. Early in my exploration, I discovered the archive of the curator and writer Adrienne Fuzee, well known in Bay Area art circles as someone who advocated fiercely and eloquently for lesbian artists, Black artists, and art that functioned outside of recognized art institutions. She lived from 1950 to 2003. My intention was always to find her a living match, but somehow it never happened. Since I knew Fuzee professionally, I would be breaking my own rule if I chose her to be my match.

But I couldn't resist returning to the six boxes in her archive, five of them filled with the evidence of her extensive creative work. In two boxes, manila folders labeled with artist names held slides of each artist's work along with a resume. One day, I found my name on a folder tab, and inside, my slides and resume from two decades back. There was something satisfying but also uncanny about finding myself in the archive; it occurred to me then that Fuzee might be my match after all. Since I created the rules, I could certainly re-invent them now.

I met Fuzee when she curated my work into her 2002 show *Jewels in a Jewel Box*. I spoke on a panel with her, one sponsored by the organization she co-founded, Lesbians in the Visual Arts. What I remember now is that I disagreed with the other speakers and most of the small audience about what they viewed as the unique and identifiable nature of lesbian art. Provocatively, I claimed that a straight man could create lesbian art without it necessarily being obvious. This was in the days when "essentialism" versus "social construction" was a critical debate in my queer circles. It seemed as if everyone else at this event believed fervently in an essentially recognizable lesbian aesthetic. And so it is that I both admired Fuzee and disagreed with her at times.

Recently, I unearthed a folder I'd forgotten about. It is overflowing with copies I made of Fuzee's writings—articles, curatorial statements, opinion pieces, college papers, fragments of lectures, a few news clippings. A script I wrote for a visual presentation about Fuzee, given at the GLBT Historical Society sometime in 2010, is also in this folder. At that event, I projected images of her text and artifacts while I spoke of her ideas, about the important niche she carved out nationally as one of the only African American lesbian curators. I showed enlarged quotations from a few of her speeches, articles, and curatorial statements. Here is a small sampling:

As a Black Female artist, I experience the forces of censorship and repression in ways that are so personally intimate and internalized, that for me to participate in a discussion of censorship requires a monumental effort. . . . Censorship is not an orphan—its father is power, its mother is religion, its siblings are repression, silence, and denial. All existing in a dynamic of dysfunction that recognizes my essential otherness and requires me to smother myself so that I may receive their "love" and be accepted.

Perhaps out of a deep-seated sense of ennui, art academicians and theorists have begun to examine, appreciate, and extol the vigorous and passionate art being produced by marginalized members of the art community. (Gay men in particular have reaped financial and critical awards for their work.) Somehow lost in all this clamor and acclaim is the work of African American Lesbian artists. For reasons that range from the mundane to the misunderstood, Lesbian art is often haphazardly categorized as blatantly sexual or overtly political, a factor that may inhibit African American Lesbian artists from identifying themselves as such. In short there is no cachet to touting one's Lesbian status.

BLOOD & DARKNESS is an all-woman show and a multi-media exhibit of artworks that emerge from each woman's acknowledgement of the internal, psychic, and artistic realities that exist and seek expression because of the powerful forces of blood and darkness. One charac-teristic that these works have in common is a certain shamelessness and courage as each artist confronts the primal forces, not to create "cunt art," but rather to create art that is in itself a manifestation of the powers and realities that transcend the work-a-day world.

HARAMBEE is an exhibit of artwork by contemporary Bay Area African American artists which seeks to describe, at this moment, the landscape and new horizons of African American aesthetics. The works of the talented artists participating in Harambee are the signposts and waystations of this new landscape. And the nature of this work is explosive—set notions about African American art must be left at the border.

I also found a copy of a news clipping from the *San Francisco Bay Area Reporter* (*BAR*), dated May 1, 2003, with an appeal for funds: "Few in the queer art world haven't heard of Adrienne Fuzee, the acclaimed art activist, cultural historian, and curator. . . . A sufferer of diabetes, Fuzee is currently experiencing a severe health crisis, friends said. She has lost vision in one of her eyes, and her left leg below the knee has been amputated." I remember thinking this appeal might be the most personal reference in her archive and wondered, Where are the diary entries, the love letters? What about a few casual snapshots or images from the shows she curated? I was looking for the Fuzee I didn't know, some clue to her more private thoughts, a way to feel a closer personal connection to her. At this point, I asked myself: Who created this archive? Who decided what to include, and where is the rest of her life?

With my third or fourth visit to Fuzee's archive, I discovered that I had overlooked a lot of personal material. Little snippets of poetry were scattered in dozens of folders, filled with references to freezing, darkness, death, despair, and the need for safe harbor.

WE are living in a dark winter of denial, when frosty winds howl in a night shatteringly bright with distant stars as we huddle around a sputtering fire of the last logs on earth. WE are living in a dark winter of denial, awaiting a springtime that exists only in our memories, consuming the last crumbs of autumn's lean harvest, eating our grain seed. WE are living in a dark winter of denial, teaching our children little of value, having learned little ourselves about the true tools of survival.

I found pages filled with aphorisms, guides to peace and serenity, to more financial security, to the lifting of depression. She kept a small notebook and filled each lined page with a diary entry. One read: "November 23. Today so much good happened that it was evidence of the rightness of my elated feelings when I woke this morning. I was elated despite my current $situation. There's so much to pay off. And I'm working as fast as I can!" This simple entry reminds me that curators I have known and worked with have most often been white women with personal financial security to offset an unstable profession. I am reminded just what an uphill struggle Fuzee endured to forge her visionary ideas as a working-class Black lesbian.

Toward the end of my presentation about Fuzee, I shifted gears. This is from my script:

I am feeling uncomfortable with this material, uncomfortable with presenting Adrienne to you, uncertain about how to select and how to offer context for her complexity. Like the person who donated her archive, I am filtering, selecting excerpts that can only be hints. I need to acknowledge my subjectivity and the realization that all this feels inadequate. I am part of this picture, and Adrienne's history and her views about art and politics and community resonate as familiar within my life. We are the same generation. I find contradictions in her writing, words I judge as utopian and highly romantic, presentations of lesbian art that make me cringe. I stop myself from analyzing, from the pressure to clearly place Adrienne in the canon of my experience. Just these fragments, a few of her words, no conclusions, no completion.

There was one more box in Fuzee's archive, box 6. It is filled with a colorful array of clothing: a beret designed like an artist palette, a t-shirt with an abstract artwork, and a pair of hip, well-worn low boots made for long narrow feet. Also, a clipboard with her name taped to the clamp. These items were more tangible, more visual, and they spoke to me emotionally. These are items that touched her skin, things that I had seen her wear and carry. Fuzee was an intellectual force of nature, and boxes 1–5 revealed many of her intricate ideas and ways of thinking. But in this box, I found her body.

My San Francisco

Several archives took me back to my early life in San Francisco during the 1970s and 1980s. Newly arrived from the East Coast in 1973, I survived a fraught pilgrimage from Boston with five other lesbians, all of us barely on speaking terms by the time we crossed the Bay Bridge in the fog. In between job and apartment searches, we eventually settled in and began to explore the plethora of gay venues in our gay mecca. Aside from an amazing selection of lesbian bars— Peg's Place and Scott's Pit were my favorite hangouts—we would save up to go to gay piano bar restaurants, places like the Fickle Fox and the Mint, where you could get a good steak and listen to lounge music. I remember being treated with a somewhat aloof respect by the older gay male clientele, also there for a good meal, a cocktail, and some live piano. Larry DeCeasar's archive, his Liberace-like attire and performance, brought back these evenings vividly. Did he play any of those nights? I don't recall, but it also took me back to the year before that when I earned the money to relocate to California by working as a topless go-go dancer in the area of downtown Boston called the Combat Zone. These were straight bars, yet queerness infiltrated each one— my own as I danced in female drag, weighed down with makeup, wig, and false eyelashes—and that of other queer dancers, including Holly, who flirted with me outrageously and let me know she strapped her dick between her legs. DeCeasar's world conjured these bars too, leaving me with an affection for him not unlike the feelings Luciano Chessa expressed for his match. For the *Archivi Migranti* exhibit in Bologna, Italy, I re-created DeCeasar's archive in a transparent archive box in which I placed brand new silver sequined gloves, identical to DeCeasar's and readily available on the internet.

When I looked through Jo Daly's archive, her disagreement with Dianne Feinstein about a Mitchell Brothers porn film made me recall my own relationship to the Mitchell Brothers' Tenderloin movie theater. I was working for United Parcel Service (UPS) as a package driver in the mid-1970s, and for about a year 895 O'Farrell Street was on my delivery route. Bored with endless packages, stressed by long hours, I tried to imagine what was in those packages—maybe film reels, maybe promotional materials, maybe concession items. What is still vivid now, though, is how once my delivery was completed at the front desk, I would make a detour down a long hallway in the back to the theater itself, where I would watch fragments of films in the dark. No one seemed to notice me in my dirt-brown UPS uniform as I took in scenes of *Behind the Green Door* with Marilyn Chambers and of

Linda Lovelace in *Deep Throat*. This felt like a perk of the job, and I knew by then how to make up the carefully policed time under UPS management surveillance. My interest in and identification with porn stemmed from my time in the Combat Zone of Boston. While I was no fan of the sexist exploitation that built the Mitchell Brothers' lucrative empire, my own memories of raids at Jacques, my first queer bar, located in downtown Boston a few blocks from where I go-go danced, were still fresh. That was in the early seventies, a time when bars in Mafia-controlled neighborhoods still had ways to signal patrons when a vice squad raid was imminent—flashing overhead lights on and off, pushing a buzzer, turning on a blinking red light under the bar. My friends and I would rush outside, dash through back alleys, and regroup at prearranged spots. Daly's sympathy for porn, had I known, would have no doubt warmed me to her. I would have enjoyed regaling her with tales from my brief flirtation with the sex industry.

Claude Schwob's archive connects to my present life in San Francisco and to the neighborhood where I've lived for twenty-two years. I think of him when I walk near the entry gate to Bayview Hunters Point, a piece of land on the eastern shore of the city that once housed the U.S. Naval Radiological Defense Laboratory (NRDL), where Schwob worked for over twenty years as one of the nation's foremost experts on radiation. I think of him now when I walk my dog, Otis, on a wild tract of shoreline called India Basin Open Space, one of only a few tidal salt marsh wetlands in the city. There is a paved trail, but to really explore the area, we scramble across thicketed fields with odd irregular dirt mounds and slide down uneven sand trails to a rocky shore that has views of container ships stranded in the bay. At the end of our walk yesterday, I noticed a "No Trespassing" sign on the area we had just exited, and another sign on a fence that reads:

"Caution: Potential buried hazardous materials. No ground disturbance allowed without approval." A few blocks away, I see the sign "Warning: Entering this area can expose you to hazardous chemicals known to the State of California to cause cancer and birth defects or other reproductive harm." Someone has scratched out the words "hazardous chemicals" and inserted "sexual desire," rendering the warning oddly humorous.

But the implications of these signs are far from humorous, and they trace back to Schwob's work. The NRDL was formed in 1946 to manage testing, decontamination, and disposition of U.S. Navy ships contaminated by the Operation Crossroads nuclear tests in the Pacific. The government lab oversaw the dumping of huge amounts of contaminated sand and acid into San Francisco Bay after they were used in attempts to clean irradiated ships. Today, the former shipyard site is still being decontaminated; it has been split into multiple parcels to allow the navy to declare them clean and safe for redevelopment separately. On my walks, I see billboards and trailers with prominent "Lennar Corporation" signs, the developer who has built and sold hundreds of new condominium units in the area. A number of regulators, activists, and cleanup workers claim that the site is still heavily contaminated and that the company contracted to handle the cleanup and testing, Tetra Tech, has repeatedly violated established protocols and deliberately falsified radiation test results to indicate that there is little remaining radiation. Employees who have attempted to force workers to perform radiation tests as required have been fired. In May 2018, two former supervisors involved in the cleanup pleaded guilty to falsifying soil sample results. In January 2019, the U.S. Justice Department sued Tetra Tech, accusing the engineering company of submitting false billing claims to the U.S. Navy that were based on falsified soil and building test data. In July 2019, the San Francisco Office of Community Investment and Infrastructure Commission approved initial plans for the construction of more homes at Hunters Point Naval Shipyard, citing the California Department of Public Health's certification that the area is clean and safe for residents.

As I face the water, Otis and I watch and listen to a symphony of gulls and pelicans; I spot two white egrets dipping their long beaks in the shallows. As we leave the wetland and cross Innes Avenue, I look up at rows and rows of newly constructed housing. I can see children and dogs playing in streets and yards, clothing hanging from lines, people eating on stoops and in the outdoor dining area of two restaurants. Another area of India Basin is being developed as a playground and picnic area, and I walk there too. Since the end of World War II, Bayview Hunters Point has been a historically Black community in which the rates of environmental diseases like asthma and cancer are high. I think again about Schwob, about his chemical expertise in radiation, and I wonder what his job duties were exactly and what he thought about as he worked. He lived to be ninety in the year 2000, a time when neighborhood contamination issues had started to enter the news. I think about environmental racism.

The Second World War and My Queer Ancestors

Several archives make me think about my parents, both of whom died in the waning days of the *LINEAGE* project. More through Lauren Crux's investigation than from my own connection to Janny MacHarg's archive, I feel Mac-Harg's stamp on the world. Now, at seventy-three, I would attend that conference on old lesbians, the one both she and Sally Rosen Binford helped organize in 1989. I might even propose a workshop. I also relate to MacHarg's early leftist history, hinted at in one photograph showing a young Mac-Harg marching in a picket line on a New York sidewalk, carrying a sign with the words "Protest the Slaughter of Spain's Underground Fighters." This was her generation's equivalent to my antiwar, antiracism, and feminist/queer activism. Having had parents who were born just five years earlier than MacHarg, ones who confronted me with considerable homophobia, and considerable terror about my lefty politics, I am deeply moved by posthumously meeting someone of their generation more like me. Growing up, I certainly did not meet or have adults in my life who could understand me across our difference. I did not have a Janny MacHarg as a role model. My retroactive desire to have known her is palpable.

Helen Harder was born the same year as my parents. The extent of my connection to this particular archive came as a surprise, and not just because of my historical crush. She seemed more directly connected to my life, and, at some point, I imagined Harder meeting my parents, Oli and Kay. In this three-way familial fantasy, I would break the ice by saying, "You were all born the same year, 1918. All of you were part of World War II. Dad—you and Helen were both simulator flight instructors. And Mom—you worked on the Army Air Force base in Marfa, Texas, which put you in proximity with all the flight instructors!"

I would ask Mom and Dad, "What do you think of Helen? She might be more like me than you, Mom—a difficult subject for you, I realize. I think you would like her, Dad." I think of their wedding photo—Mom in a serious brown velour suit with pink neck ruffle, Dad in his Army Air Force uniform with a cocked envelope hat. A wartime wedding in West Texas. And I want to say to my mother, "That suit you wore is my inheritance, my lineage, the blood lineage I was born into. It hangs in my front closet now. It means something, and I understand why you were upset not to have grandkids from your five offspring. Sorry about that. I thought about it a few decades ago, but you were horrified at the thought of me raising a kid. I suppose you would judge Helen too, with her illegitimate bastard son who inherited her 1940s-era vibrator. But she is my lineage too, the part you could never give me or acknowledge or even talk about. And that's something."

Finding Jiro Onuma's archive reminded me that in 1942 my mother made a solo trip as a young single woman from West Texas to Sacramento, California, staying with relatives. When I asked her about this trip, instead of recounting tales of adventure, she recalled the shocking sight of Japanese American families loaded down with possessions as they boarded a troop train poised to leave Sacramento. For where? When I look at the photos of young Onuma in the 1920s and 1930s, I am reminded of snapshots I have of my Yankee father in wartime, stationed in West Texas. In these photos, my father is dark and slight, so slight that he was under the army's weight limit of 120 pounds. In one of my father's photos, his reclining effeminate pose on a rock is almost identical to a pose Onuma took at about the same age in a San Francisco park. My father, whose own father emigrated from Canada to Vermont and became a small-town Episcopal minister. A very different immigration story.

Unstable Bodies

Disability played a significant role in my family history, and still does. When I opened Diane Hugaert's box, its contents instantly connected to my relationship as the older sibling and now guardian of a severely disabled sister. It brought up protective and uneasy feelings that are ancient, early memories of defending my sister against the taunts of other kids and of performing disability in my own eccentric ways. In my pre-teen socially awkward years, I sometimes walked around pigeon-toed or limped with all the subtlety of a peg-legged pirate. To impress and scare my friends, I painted lurid outbreaks of poison ivy across my left arm with chalk and crayons. Sometimes I'd speak with a lisp or mimic the Texas drawl my mother had willfully erased by the time I was born. In these ways, disability and otherness became inseparable from my own emerging identity. The residue of this childhood sense of mission made me feel protective of Hugaert; I wanted to make sure to match her with someone who would treat her highly personal material with understanding and empathy. As the participant Dominika Bednarska developed her relationship to Hugaert, launching a powerful dialogue across their shared body experiences, my connection to this archive intensified. My feelings of having trespassed as I pored over her anguished and vulnerable writings grew more acute.

Learning about Jessica Barshay's struggle with invisible disabilities so severe that she ended her life with intention also recalled my family of origin. My three younger brothers, born prematurely two minutes apart, experienced compromised health starting in infancy. In adulthood, they have in varying degrees suffered from a span of invisible illnesses not unlike Barshay's, ones that at times have affected their ability to function. The phrase she coined in an essay in her archive, "active unwillingness to know," comes back to me now as I recognize the ways I have tuned out my brothers' complaints, dismissing them as hyperbole. Me, the only queer kid in a family of seven, and yet the only one living in a so-called normal body. I cringe as I realize I might have responded to Barshay in the same way.

I don't remember exactly when I learned the word *suicide*, but its shadow crossed my life soon after birth, the year my father's middle brother, John, died. After that, his youngest brother, Albro, visited us. I can still picture him standing at our kitchen counter, rubbing his index finger on the Formica surface, and throwing his voice in some way that seemed like utter magic. Uncle Albro never returned, and, at some point, I learned he had died too, maybe in a car. There was a vague silence my young curiosity could not brook as my questions collided with my father's anger, anger that was abrupt and harsh. The silence was thick and offered no way to penetrate its walls.

I think it was in my early teen years that I first understood that Uncle Albro had ended his own life, as had John before him. Two out of three sons of an artist and a stern small-town Vermont minister. In my early sleuthing, I somehow found out that John hung himself and that Albro shut himself up in a car, turned on the ignition, and hosed in carbon monoxide. I knew that he waited until just after my grandmother Edith, who I am named after and with whom I shared a bedroom, died. Much later, I found a diary from this period filled with my mother's difficult scrawl. In one entry she wrote, "The state police called today." Three days later, "Albro found in car." Years later, I found a journal kept by my grandfather and went to these same dates. In cryptic sentences, he wrote about the weather, about how the garden was that day, about taking his dog, Wimpy, for a walk, about this and that.

Suicide became one of my most intense curiosities, along with disability and adoption. This fascination has continued into adulthood, past my parents' deaths, to my present preoccupation with the archives of the dead. And this is what led me to the life of Sally Rosen Binford, a woman with a fascinating history that touched the lives of several people I know. The fact that she intentionally ended her life just before turning seventy, made me yearn to know more and led me to match her to someone who would find out more.

The good-bye letter Binford wrote to her friends shocked me. I have a hard time reconciling Binford's suicide, coming as it did when her life was reportedly full, happy, and healthy, not young and miserable like that of my uncles. It seemed like a proactive suicide that looked forward to what she didn't want to endure—old age—instead of to present or past misery. As a late bloomer in so many ways, as student, artist, teacher, and now writer, I think about my hopes for life in my seventies and beyond, all the things I still want to experience and do. In my life and that of people I'm close to, so much has become possible in our senior years, including, in my case, a mended relationship to my parents, who lived into their nineties. Had they died at seventy, I would not have made peace with my homophobic mother, nor finally asked my father about his brothers when he could respond without defensiveness and anger. The fact that Binford seemed to consider seventy too old to endure strikes me as tragic, far too controlling, and—when I remember MacHarg's song "Aging Is Not for Sissies"—perhaps even cowardly.

Spinsters

H. Drew Crosby's archive reminded me of my intense curiosity as a kid about the single women in my parents' circle, mostly grade-school teacher colleagues of my dad. They were Crosby's generation, and I knew a couple of them lived with another woman. Miss Andino, my second grade teacher, dressed fashionably, wore exotic jewelry, and laughed uproariously. I remember inventing noble romances for her, handsome fiancés who died tragically in the war, leaving her alone and too sad to marry someone else. In the same period, my girlfriends and I would spend hours playing old maid, the card game in which whoever is left holding the ugly spinster loses. She was pictured with a warty nose, high collar, and severe hair—a cross between a witch and a Victorian prude. Later, in high school, with the understanding that sex and marriage were not the same thing, I obsessed over whether Miss Andino had ever had sex.

Years later when she died, Isabelle Andino left my parents a box of snapshots, some elegant objects from her travels around the world, and a beautiful gold ring with ruby stone jutting out, like a crown. This, they said, had been given to her by her very dear friend Bea, short for Beatrice, I think. I had always heard about Bea, but never remember seeing or meeting her. My father is the one who lifted this ring out of its delicate red velvet case, holding it aloft as though to offer it to me. I examined it respectfully, feeling an emotional symbolism in his gesture, a potential passing on of the torch of supposed spinsterhood. Inside the band I noticed minuscule scrolled letters, a barely discernible script of initials with periods: I.O.E.F.L. Neither of my parents had any idea what this meant, but I imagined a secret love code between Isabelle and Bea. I wanted that ring and said so in no uncertain words.

What happened next was so strange, I feel a shiver even now. My father returned the ruby ring to its satin-lined box and started hedging. "What if one of your brothers gets engaged? This could be a ring for him to present to his fiancée." I was flabbergasted. Here I sat, oldest daughter, unmarried lesbian, former second grade pupil of Miss Andino, expressing a clear interest in the ring I thought he was offering, a ring with absolutely no link to our family lineage, and my father was imagining a hypothetical future bride for one of my unmarried forty-something younger triplet brothers, who never even had her as a teacher! I was so hurt, so insulted, words initially failed me. How could they be so tone-deaf and so cruel, so absolutely unaware of the painful symbolism in this simple refusal? It didn't take long for self-righteous fury to take over, and I let out a torrent of passionate invective: "How can you sit there and treat me like I'm invisible, like I'm not worth as much because I never married? And all in comparison to your wishful thinking about an imaginary fiancée one of 'the boys,' not even a specific brother, might someday have?" Tears burst down my face, and I felt like a sixteen-year-old again, helpless and indignant, mistreated. The ancient words from my childhood, "It's not fair," once again erupted like underground lava. My tantrum prodded my father to get up and leave, while my mother retreated into a cold, frightening silence.

In the end, I got the ring. It sits in my jewelry box, forgotten most of the time, too large for any of my fingers. My father later apologized, using brief, clipped words that nevertheless meant the world to me. My mother refused to budge from her denial of my issues, but I got a strange flash of insight into something from her past, something that had numbed her long ago. Her extreme refusal to deal with my emotions seemed less like power over me than like something that had a grip on her, something she herself had no conscious awareness of. I'll never know the basis for my hunch; it was never something she and I would speak about in our more intimate moments. It was a secret I glimpsed occasionally, a secret as locked into the past as the delicately scripted code etched on the inside of the ruby ring, my legacy from Miss Isabelle Andino.

It would have been easy and predictable for H. Drew Crosby's and Marion Pietsch's lives to be obscured under silence and mystery too, but for a few chance events. They didn't identify as lesbians any more than did the spinsters in my childhood, who may or may not have loved women. But it is noteworthy that Crosby's obituary makes specific reference to "long-time companion Marion Pietsch." I wonder, Who wrote "long-time companion" and would Crosby have approved? Who made sure she and Pietsch were buried together at Mount Tamalpais cemetery? Kevin Bentley has no idea. He lost touch with Crosby soon after his lover Richard reluctantly disclosed his HIV status to her, at which point she cut Richard off cold, saying, "Go talk to my lawyer." Here was a woman who had worked in hospitals for years yet could not tolerate the specter of sickness, especially AIDS, in someone she cared about. Richard died the next year, in 1992. My parting question for Bentley when we met recently was about how the video oral history came to be in the archive. It was the participant Terry Berlier who first imagined that Crosby, with her intense fear of exposure, would not want to have anything to do with a queer archive.

And yet, at age eighty, Crosby willingly allowed her two gay male friends to record her stories, to expose her racism and other faults, to be vulnerable in her own way. In the end, Crosby gave Bentley permission to donate the video to the GLBT Historical Society, a kind of late coming out. I'm remembering her phrase "I won't say any more," referring to her Black patient, which I interpret as some kind of awareness that her racism would not be acceptable to these younger white men. To further complicate the unknowable, I found a snapshot in the archive showing Crosby, late in life, standing next to a seated Black woman of about her age who Bentley remembered as her good friend Elsie. Their eyes focus on something out of camera view, and Crosby is in the act of handing Elsie a teacup on a saucer, slightly tipped, as though she might lose her balance and spill the contents. I mention this, aware that it sounds like the "some of my best friends are . . ." excuse. But, in contrast to Berlier's desire to distance from Crosby, I feel no need to make excuses for her or to redeem her character. My desire, rather, is to allow the few artifacts she left behind to speak with all their inconclusiveness and contradictions.

The last time my parents visited me in California, my father unfolded a family tree chart on the kitchen table. It was a work in progress, a rough draft so enormous it spilled over the table edges, and we had to maneuver around it. The older generations branched out with names that were barely familiar to me, and I noticed under several boxes—ones with limbs going in but not out—the word *spinster* in parentheses. Neither of my father's brothers, who died young, married, yet there was nothing to indicate their bachelor status. My generation's row of boxes similarly had no modifying labels; they looked unfinished compared to the rows above. I asked my father, "So Dad, what are you going to put under my name? What about Jo Ellen's [my sister]? What about the boys? And what about your brothers?" This was my perfect entrance to once again bring up the idea of invisible and undiscussed family issues: sexuality, suicide, disability. I took his silent shrug to mean I'd gotten through in some tiny way. When he sent me a much-reduced copy of the final product a year later, the word *spinster* had been deleted; the boxes with no exit branches stood on their own, unexplained.

Two Fathers, One a Woman

This connection between my parents, especially my father, and an archive was surprisingly most intense in relation to Veronica Friedman. In my studio at an artist's residency in Wyoming shortly after my father died in 2013, I pinned all the notes he left behind to a wall, alongside copies of all Friedman's notes. One hundred or so square feet of odd-shaped papers, handwritten lists, charts, and graphs. When I opened the window, the notes would flutter and dance in the breeze. Two fathers, one who became a woman, both with somewhat obsessive notation habits, both concerned with scientific truth. Friedman questioned that truth and questioned her family's rejection of her true gender. She wrote about love and love lost on those napkins. I wanted my dad and Friedman to meet. I wanted my dad's huge archive to share memory objects with Friedman's slim one. I became a detective, searching for details in both lives—the truncated life of Friedman, and the long life of my reticent science-teacher father. I imagined introducing them and speculated about how my dad might have related to Friedman and Friedman to him. I imagined gifts from my dad to Friedman, offerings. And I searched for people who had known Friedman.

Barbara McBane's idea, as she wrote in her essay, was to respect the absences in Friedman's archive, to make work rooted in the ephemerality of the available information. I loved this idea in theory, but another urge swept over me, and I couldn't resist my desire to know more. It was true back then and it's true today as I write this. For our collaboration, I agreed to McBane's sensibility about Friedman and kept my detective work out of the picture as I focused on my father's archive. But independent of our work together, I indulged my desire to find out more.

I looked up every address referenced in Friedman's slim archive, hoping to get a literal sense of places she called home at different times. I wrote two letters by hand, one to her brother, Barry Friedman, and another to the person who donated her archive in 1994, Robert Morgan Lawrence, co-founder with Carol Queen of the Center for Sex & Culture. Writing to Barry Friedman brought back a similar sense of trespass I had felt when I draped cloth on old gravestones, using chalk to bring up the carved text. Who was I, a total stranger, to write to these people who had been close to Veronica Friedman, asking all my nosy questions?

These efforts on my part were unsuccessful until 2013 when I tracked down Joy Christi Przestwor on Facebook, the lesbian who was named conservator while Friedman lay in a coma with a brain tumor at Herrick Hospital in Oakland, California, in 1986. Przestwor responded in an email: "I have photos, tapes, and VHS video of 'V's' 40th birthday party. We were lovers for a few years and dear, deeply spiritual friends from the moment we set eyes on one another. . . . I am thrilled that you are doing this research and will do my best to add information to your work. Veronica was a special presence on this planet and continues to be one of those inter-dimensional persons in my life. She has never left my life from the moment she entered it. Our story of sharing life and all it has to offer is a delightful journey of awareness and love."

Then, out of the blue in late 2019, I got a phone call from a woman who identified herself as Friedman's daughter, Shelly, and referred to herself as "one of the kids who rejected her." We talked for a while, and she wrote to me in two different emails:

> Every now and then I google my father's name. Veronica Friedman, née Ron Friedman. It's in vain hopes to find information I don't already know. Today I stumbled upon your work juxtaposing her with another gentleman. Your father, maybe?
>
> Anyway, I have seen the small collection of items belonging to her left at the [GLBT history] museum in SF. There is no whole picture of the person she was in that box. It is so far from a complete picture. Unfortunately, I cannot complete it as I was only in 1st grade when my parents divorced. But I do believe it is important that the family be taken into account when creating your hypothesis about the person she was. I strongly believe that you

need to take into account that the items in that box were not put there by herself. Rather, they were donated by someone who held onto that box for some time and who most likely chose items that would be the most provocative. I know this because there was only one letter from a 7-year-old version of myself asking him to change back. 7. What 7-year-old wouldn't want that? And yet I wrote oh so many more letters than that. Where are they?

. . . When I first found out about the archive, I told my uncle [Barry Friedman]. He went to check it out before I did and warned me that there may be some stuff that I wouldn't want to know in them. He was right, but I knew I needed to see it all for myself. I even asked if I could take the originals home and leave copies as I was a direct descendant, and no one had ever asked if I wanted these items to be donated. Of course, I was shot down. So, I ended up with copies of some of the pieces I felt I wanted. It is still quite upsetting to know that my father was given away, so to speak, without being consulted. That there are strangers out there that may think they know her based on what was in that box. Or worse yet, that they may be judging me as part of the cause of her unhappiness (since I couldn't accept that he had become a she) without considering my age or that there were other letters, that I loved my father with all my heart and . . . still do.

I do greatly appreciate hearing that you do not presume to know my father after reading her archives. Thank you for knowing there is more to the story.

I've attached a photo of my father, as I knew him (as I do not have any pictures post transition). And a picture of my mother and I at my wedding 12 years ago. Another pic of my brother walking me down the aisle. And one last one of my husband and our children on the first day of school this year. Just as a reference for our family.

I was dumbstruck, in part because this was the first image I was seeing of Veronica Friedman, taken when she was still Ron. Up to that point, there was nothing in the archive to conjure what she looked like, either before or after transition. Shelly shared such a complicated web of feelings with me—a sense of loss and sadness, a degree of pride in her dad, an eagerness to clear her name of prejudice, anger at the archive itself and at the GLBT Historical Society. My reactions were complicated too—I feel sympathy for Shelly's pain and loss, and her desire to know more about her dad, . . . hadn't I embarked on a similar search for my dad? I appreciated that Shelly switched easily between gender pronouns for her dad, and I can only imagine how hard that might be for a daughter. But I also responded as a queer who is left out of the heterosexual family portrait she conjures in her family photos, a queer who relishes finding any artifacts at all of a life like Friedman's, incomplete as they may be. A queer who has more in common with Friedman than with Shelly, and who understands the trust Friedman put in nonbiological family. I know that the fact Friedman's slim archive ended up preserved at all is a small miracle.

Przestwor fell out of touch after my initial outreach, but I finally heard from her again seven years later while in the process of writing this chapter. She lives in a different state and has become a minister, and she offered to search for her cassettes and video. We met over Zoom and talked for over an hour, during which my sense of Friedman became far more multidimensional. Przestwor, who had been a nun for fifteen years, described meeting Friedman as an unlicensed massage therapist who put up notices in San Francisco gay bars. Przestwor was on a lesbian softball team and saw one of Friedman's ads in the bar where her team was celebrating a win: "If you want a massage, call me." After several false starts—Przestwor was shy and reluctant—she finally rang Friedman's doorbell on Geary Street. They sat in the apartment kitchen, ate bagels and lox, and talked for two and a half hours before the massage. Once on the massage table, Friedman said, "I need to tell you something." Przestwor replied, "I already know. You're a transgender person," and Friedman responded, "How did you know?" Their connection was strong, and they became both good friends and lovers.

Przestwor described how she and Friedman wrote poetry on napkins together over dinner. They took turns recording for each other what they called cassette letters, their life histories divided into decades. Friedman took Przestwor to SM bars and the baths, pushing every boundary she could for this ex-nun. Przestwor described Friedman in phrases like "V was a special, authentic, and generous presence. When she walked into a room, she made a difference. She helped and mentored a lot of younger trans people, always respectful of difference." Przestwor also emailed me six photos of Friedman. It was startling to suddenly see her wide smile and somewhat shy demeanor, bold and hesitant at the same time, her long curly hair, her slim figure dressed in blue jeans, except in one photo in which she wears a long white dress and has a flower in her hair. I had forgotten that I had no conventional image of Friedman, nothing outside the gender charts and graphs in her archive.

A few months later, I heard this from Przestwor: "I have GREAT news! I found all the cassette tapes and the video of V's 40th birthday party. I can put them all in the mail so you can enjoy a fuller view of V's life (as well as mine). My only request, since the material on those tapes is so intimate and personal, is that you respect that as you use it in your writing. There was nothing we held from one another as our sharing continued and our love for each other continued to grow and develop." As I write, I am waiting to receive these materials.

The collaboration with McBane, both my matching her to Friedman in the first place, and our collaborative gallery installation about Friedman and my father, brought up interesting, at times contentious, and very personal issues for both of us. Each match I have made is a three-way relationship—between me and an archive, between a person I match to their archive, and between the two of us as living collaborators. As I move in and out of possessive pronouns—my match, their archive—I think about possessiveness and responsibility in relationships. I discovered the archive first—so it's *mine* in a sense. Yet I'm giving it away to a volunteer participant in my project, which renders it *theirs*, at least for the duration of the project. Friedman's daughter wanted to own Friedman's archive and felt wronged when the GLBT Historical Society would not break its acquisition agreement to give her original documents. The irony is not lost on me: three cisgender women, two of us lesbians and one a biological daughter, all making claims on the sparse archive of a transgender woman, all feeling like our relationship to Friedman is special. I like to imagine Friedman getting a postmortem kick out of all this attention.

Who owns an archive anyway? There are legalities of course, the rules by which the institution that is home to an archive operates. And then there is historical imperative, such as stated in the mission of most archives—to preserve the records of history, and especially the records of people who have been historically elided. In my work, I have attempted to spark something else in relation to archival history: personal connection and a stake in the archive I introduce to participants—the development of a relationship between a living person and a dead person that is generative, that in a sense gives the dead person a new life, not a memorial but some other kind of extension into the present and out to a public—a community that includes both the living and the dead.

The ethics suggested by these complicated questions seem uncertain. Do we out a closeted person through their archive after they die? Do we go against the wishes of family members who wish that their queer relative's artifacts remain private? What do we the living owe the person whose relics we are studying, and what do we owe both their biological family and their identity-based family? Friedman transitioned into her gender in a very different era; the language we find in her archive is no longer current or considered trans-positive. So, I wonder what language I should use about her now. I don't have definitive answers to these and other questions. I pick my way through each project step-by-step, trying to pay attention and to do right by both living and dead collaborators.

My Untended Archive

In her late seventies, not much older than I am now, my mother was engaged in a grand inventory. Each time I visited, she would pull out reams of lined yellow legal paper, every page filled with her difficult-to-read script. She was in the process of listing all the items she and my father had acquired over fifty-odd years of marriage, a daunting task since nothing escaped the urgency of her cataloging. In her system, an antique carved chest of drawers with lion's claw feet sat comfortably in the same column, united by function, with the blond 1950s dresser where I housed my teenage sweaters. Photographs of all the siblings are listed along with miniature portraits my grandmother painted of previous generations. Artwork I sent my parents over the years is listed in the same category as tourist posters from their travels;

a delicately painted ceramic box given to them on their wedding day sits on a line directly above the ceramic yellow-glazed lion with a spaghetti-textured mane that I made in second grade. Nothing escaped these thorough yellow columns, indexes of a married life, measure of respectable accomplishment.

My task was to initial the items that interested me, the things I might want to take after my parents died. It's never been clear to me how she planned to settle competing desires among five offspring, but her intentions were admirably responsible. She did not want to leave this world with a disarray of personal effects, a burden to her children. It was her way of preparing this last stage of her life, of reflecting on her many years as wife, mother, and local history museum guide. Most of the items requiring careful historical annotation came from my father's family, things she claimed through marriage and now delegated with reverence. But she also grew generous in this process, letting me choose freely from the linens and costume jewelry that belonged to her family. I am now the proud possessor of a tablecloth that depicts the state of Texas and a rhinestone pin that is a replica of the crown Queen Elizabeth wore as a young bride. It was clearly a joy to my mother when I showed interest and gratitude in owning something that was meaningful to her. I have slowly come to understand her worst fear: that these things, the measure of her life, would end up at a flea market, sad remnants of neglect. With five middle-aged and unmarried children, no grandkids, no one to carry on the family name or legacy, what kind of home would her familiar objects occupy? What strangers would handle them in a vacuum, oblivious to their origins and history?

Apparently, I am not my mother's daughter. I have not obsessively logged my every item or figured out where things will go, how to sort them, whom to give them to before

I am too old. Hers was a task she never completed, though she worked on it for over a decade. But it is I, out of five kids, who kept those yellow-lined legal pad sheets with their cramped writing and tiny sketches that logged my mother's life accumulation, her life laid out in things. Her archiving instincts represented, I think, a desire to measure her worth in a legacy she could pass on. Five of the boxes in my closets and basement are labeled "Mom." They hold the items my brothers had no interest in—most of her things, artifacts from her childhood through her ninety-two years. Two items don't fit in the boxes: a tiny red wooden rocking chair, with crusty, peeling paint, that she sat in when she was one year old and the small blue rocking horse my father made for me when I was two.

The irony that, as an archive artist, I have done nothing to sort through my own personal archive mess does not escape me. How will I be known, remembered? Does it matter? Bill Domonkos said about not wanting to be in an archive: "I'm left with the impression that once we're gone we really don't have any control over our legacy. I hope what remains of me does not end up in an archive somewhere. I prefer to just vanish, without a trace." Unlike Domonkos, I want to leave a trace. I can't offer a postmortem guarantee to my mother, but this project has made me realize that I want younger researchers to come upon my things, the evidence of my life and my projects. I'm just not sure how to make it happen. Yes, I can organize all the stuff related to queer me for the GLBT Historical Society Archives and should start soon. But there is so much more; what do I do with the correspondence my mother inherited between Confederate soldier ancestors and family in Texas, the letters my parents tried unsuccessfully to give to a Texas historical society? What about my gravestone rubbings from a photographic project called *Quasi Lapis*? Or all the components of other art installations? What about the metal cabinet of records from my sister's medical and social history, put together by my mother? My father's botanical notebooks, the embroidered Christmas stockings from one aunt, and the crocheted doilies from another. The handmade furniture my father built, along with cutting boards and abstract sculptures? Or the clothes my mother made for me that I've stored between layers of tissue paper? I suppose if I were famous, the potential division of me and my history between institutions and the dumpster might not be an issue. So many of the archives I looked at seemed incomplete, leaving me thirsty for more artifacts, more records, more knowledge of the person across their life. This both inspires me to start sorting through my stuff, once this book is done, and daunts me in frozen stagnation. It is clear there will be no unity to my archive identity after I die.

Unstable Archives and Lineage

Everyone has a lineage—somewhere. But not all of us can touch it or talk about it. Things get in the way: poverty, exile, war, shame, silence, isolation. And if that is the case, where do we go to search for connection, to find antecedents, to identify our spot in the historical scheme of things? Community archives have become a crucial resource for preserving the most ephemeral histories. In the case of queer archives, preservation of the past is often a rescue effort against the wishes of families and communities who want to keep their privacy, or institutions interested in image control. If they are saved at all, queer artifacts are often secreted away, held in reserve until people die, left in basements, or anonymously passed on. While this shame slowly lifts, we still rely on institutions like the GLBT Historical Society to preserve evidence from our queer past.

At this point I hope it is obvious that the archive exchanges I developed for both the *LINEAGE* and the *Migrating Archives* projects do not leave empty gaps on their home shelves. If that were the case, I would have quickly become an archive outlaw, banned from archive access, my status as artist-in-residence revoked. While proud to be an archive nerd, I am not an archivist who is required to conform to archivist protocols. As an artist, I create situations in which archives can mutate into multiple forms, migrate through social exchanges, and be returned to their shelves intact. There is movement, a flux, as archives are fleshed out, visualized, and enacted by passionate intention. Normally stable historical artifacts morph with a slippage art can engender. Jiro Onuma's archive has been expanded to include the *Gay Bachelor's Japanese American Internment Camp Survival Kit* created by the artist and scholar Tina Takemoto, not as a literal donation, but existing out there in the form of objects, writing, and performance. Nomy Lamm's arrangement of a new version of Silvia Kohan's song became a refrain sung and played by two dozen musicians in a jam session at the GLBT Historical Society that Kohan would not have missed. Luciano Chessa wrote his aria based on a handwritten prayer found in Larry DeCeasar's box, and the soprano Don Tatro sang it to audiences on several occasions. Maya Manvi created the tools that might have helped Dodi Horvat re-imagine their gender in keeping with the complicated gender culture revealed in their science fiction notes. One by one these archives are spilling out their contents into a stream of new, alive public forms.

Most of the time, archives sit safely in their boxes, waiting for the occasional researcher. But as an artist, I can instigate a process in which the responses of participants form new kinds of archives, archives in motion, ones that widen our kinship networks and reflect the activism that queer collecting organizations have in common. For people whose traces are so often erased even by our biological families, omitted from official histories, or just plain lost, archives are a way of fostering our own lineage, of taking charge and imagining a future—a process that is rarely static.

The dates of the *LINEAGE* project, 2008–2014, cover a period when most of the archives I looked at included some combination of printed photographs, news clippings, promotional flyers, handwritten letters, and diaries. But what about archives submitted now and in the near future? How many and how much will be digital, sometimes entirely ephemeral? My sense of physical objects as a stand-in for a person's body would shift, rendering an archive more abstract, perhaps more like memory. There might be nothing left to touch, no reason to wear white gloves, no "there" there. Or maybe it will render a person's mortality abstract, the way that a Facebook page or other social media bit can live on in the strange immortality of a person's digital life. In *An Inventory of Losses*, Judith Schalansky writes: "Sometimes I imagine the future thus: generations to come standing baffled in front of today's data storage media, strange aluminum boxes whose contents, . . . file formats and playback devices, have become nothing but meaningless codes, and moreover ones that, as an object in themselves, exude less of an aura than the knots of an Inca quipu string, as eloquent as they are mute, or those mystifying ancient Egyptian obelisks that may commemorate triumph or tragedy, no one knows."[2]

In a physical comment book at the first *LINEAGE: Matchmaking in the Archive* exhibition, a person who signed "Berkeley," wrote: "This exhibit simultaneously enthralled and disquieted me. It is somehow both comforting and disturbing to think of a life as an archive, at once preserved and diminished. Completely beautiful work on all counts."

It was interesting to register this comment articulating the same contradictions I experienced in relation to the project, ones I still grapple with as I write this book.

Acting as an embedded artist within the GLBT Historical Society gave me a way to consciously create public frameworks for interaction with the archives. The projects I've described take me in and out of art world contexts in a way that feels right. This work has offered me a new way to be an artist, one who is arbiter of my own practice. And now I have a queer lineage. This project, this book, and all the archives I've gotten to know, have given me one.

LINEAGE: Matchmaking in the Archive provides one model for how to bring archives, our history, off the archive shelf into creative visibility. It provided a strategy to bring new people into the archive, to foster uncanny lineages, and to spark our imaginations. In this process, desire crosses time, crosses into and out from the archive, and lurks in liminal spaces between life and death. Personal archives arouse prurient curiosities, inappropriate speculations, and impossible longings—perfect provocation for art that inscribes queer history in new ways.

Acknowledgments

As a visual and conceptual artist, I have often made use of text that accompanies or merges with the materials and structure of an artwork. Sometimes, my use of words is poetic and rendered in powdered sugar. Other times a passage of text is projected in light. Or spoken by a voice actor. Or burned into wood or cut out of a photograph. It has been strange and at times unsettling to create a text that is rendered solely on a laptop screen and then printed on paper, text that must cohere and make sense on the scale of a book.

To accomplish this, I have relied on my friends and colleagues who are writers and readers for advice. Their feedback has been nothing short of enlightening; at times, I felt like I was attending my own private graduate writing program. I owe a debt of gratitude to the people who read versions at different stages, offered insightful comments, or just simply encouraged me when I was questioning why I ever embarked on this adventure.

First, a huge thank you to all of the *LINEAGE* match participants, who threw yourselves whole heartedly into the project, then returned in memory to give me your updated insights. Your indelible stories form the heart of this book.

Thank you, Jeffrey Escoffier, longtime friend and fellow editor on the Q+ Public series. You were a careful and perceptive reader from the early stages. I almost always left our

Monday morning Zoom meetings feeling energized and inspired. Your recent untimely death has been devastating.

Thank you, Kimberly Guinta at Rutgers University Press, who has fostered and encouraged the Q+ Public series, including this book, from the start. Without you, my book would not be.

Thank you, Camille Norton, amazing poet, participant in the *LINEAGE* project, and longtime friend. You pored over my chapters with such patience more than once, helping me figure out how to sculpt the shape of this book.

Thank you, Julian Carter, fellow Q+ Public editorial board member and friend. You offered delightful and perceptive responses both to my early versions in our writing exchange and to my more final versions.

Thank you, Lauren Crux, longtime friend and co-conspirator on several art projects, including *LINEAGE*, for helpful feedback early on.

Thank you, Mickey Eliason, writer and educator, friend and participant in my *OUT/LOOK & the Birth of the Queer* project. Our writing feedback exchanges, your attention to detail, taught me a lot.

Thank you, Jan Freeman, professional editor, who helped me recognize the different strands of my book.

Thank you, Fran Bartkowski, Joan Hirschfeld, Maya Manvi, Rachel Katz, and Joan Balter. Each of you took the time to read parts of the book, and each of you in your own way gave me the encouragement I needed.

Thank you, Don Romesburg, for enthusiastically shepherding the original *LINEAGE: Matchmaking in the Archive* project from the get-go; without your trust and support from within the GLBT Historical Society, my artist's residency would not have happened, and the project would have been something else entirely.

Thank you, Kevin Bentley, for meeting with me in person, and Rev. Joy Christi Przestwor for meeting with me on Zoom. The new information you both generously shared about the archives of H. Drew Crosby and Veronica Friedman brought them to life for me in profound ways.

Last of all, thank you to my pandemic pup, Otis, who has been the best kind of warm and fuzzy distraction while working on this book.

Notes

Preface

1. Walter Benjamin, *Selected Writings, vol. 4, 1938–1940* (Cambridge, MA: Belknap Press of Harvard University Press, 2006), 48.

Part 2   Nineteen Conversations with the Dead

1. Tina Takemoto, "Notes on Internment Camp," *Art Journal* 72, no. 2 (2013): 55.
2. Tina Takemoto, "Looking for Jiro Onuma: A Queer Meditation on the Incarceration of Japanese Americans during World War II," *GLQ: A Journal of Lesbian and Gay Studies* 20, no. 3 (2014): 241–275.
3. Alan Bérubé, *Coming Out under Fire: The History of Gay Men and Women in World War II* (1990; Chapel Hill: University of North Carolina Press, 2010).
4. Janny MacHarg, "Niche Picking," in "Old Lesbians/Dykes," *Sinister Wisdom* 53 (1994): 59.
5. Pat Parker, *Womanslaughter*, (Diana Press, 1978): 48
6. Julie Enszer, ed., *Sister Love: The Letters of Audre Lorde and Pat Parker 1974–1989* (New York: A Midsummer Night's Press, 2018).
7. Susie Bright, "Checking Out," *Susie Bright's Journal*, October 12, 2006, http://susiebright.blogs.com/susie_brights_journal_/2006/10/checking_out.html.

8. Liz M. Quinlan, "'. . . and His Wife Sally': The Binford Legacy and Uncredited Work in Archaeology" (paper presented at the Eighty-Fourth Annual Meeting of the Society for American Archaeology, Albuquerque, NM, 2019).

9. Susie Bright, "From Tight Sweaters to the Pentagon Papers," *Susie Bright's Journal*, May 16, 2008, https://susiebright.blogs.com/susie_brights_journal_/2008/05/sally-binford-n.html.

10. Bright, "Tight Sweaters."

11. Sally Rosen Binford, "Myths and Matriarchies," in *The Politics of Women's Spirituality: Essays on the Rise of Spiritual Power within the Feminist Movement*, ed. Charlene Spretnak (New York: Anchor Books/Doubleday, 1982), 541–549.

12. Bright, "Tight Sweaters."

13. Bright, "Tight Sweaters."

14. Bright, "Tight Sweaters."

15. Bright, "Checking Out."

16. Kevin Bentley, *Let's Shut Out the World* (2005; New York: Chelsea Station Editions, 2016), 146.

17. Bentley, *Shut Out*, 139.

18. Robert L. Dickinson, "The Gynecology of Homosexuality," in *Sex Variants: A Study of Homosexual Patterns*, by George W. Henry (1941; New York: Paul B. Hoeber, 1948), 1078.

19. Barbara McBane, "Veronica's Ghost: Queer Time and the Porous Archive," *Art Journal* 72, no. 2 (2013): 58–63.

20. McBane, "Veronica's Ghost," 59–62.

21. McBane, "Veronica's Ghost," 63.

22. Jessica Barshay, "Another Strand of Our Diversity: Some Thoughts from a Feminist Therapist with Severe Chronic Illness," in *Women with Disabilities: Found Voices*, ed. Mary E. Willmuth and Lillian Holcomb (New York: Routledge, 1993), 159–169.

23. Barshay, "Another Strand," 159.

24. Sabine Russell, obituary for Jo Daly, SFGATE, October 6, 1997, https://www.sfgate.com/news/article/Jo-Daly-51-First-Lesbian-on-S-F-Police-Panel-2803150.php.

25. Britannica ProCon.org, "Jo Daly Biography," October 23, 2009, https://medicalmarijuana.procon.org/source-biographies/jo-daly/.

26. Russell, Jo Daly.

27. Living in Leather, "Cynthia Slater," July 12, 2022, http://livinginleather.net/cynthia-slater.html.

28. Jack Fritscher Drummer Feature Article, "The Janus Society: Kiss and Don't Tell, Cynthia Slater and the Catholic Priest," July 12, 2022, http://www.jackfritscher.org/Drummer/Issues/027/Janus%20Society.html.

29. SFGATE, Delfin Vigil, "Trevor Hailey—Started Castro Gay History Tours," June 15, 2007, https://www.sfgate.com/bayarea/article/Trevor-Hailey-started-Castro-gay-history-tours-2555870.php.

30. San Francisco Bay Times, "Trevor Hailey's Legacy Thrives in the Castro," July 12, 2022, https://sfbaytimes.com/trevor-haileys-legacy-thrives-castro/.

31. Bill Lipsky, Ph.D., "Rainbow Honor Walk: Passionate Activist George Choy," San Francisco Bay Times, July 13, 2022, https://sfbaytimes.com/rainbow-honor-walk-passionate-activist-george-choy/.

32. Lipsky, "Rainbow Honor."

33. "Silvia Kohan Obituary," Los Angeles Times, July 13, 2022, https://www.legacy.com/us/obituaries/latimes/name/silvia-kohan-obituary?n=silvia-kohan&pid=1138618.

Part 4   Lineages of Desire

1. Molly McGarry, *Ghosts of Futures Past* (Berkeley: University of California Press, 2008), 16, 156.

2. Judith Schalansky, *An Inventory of Losses*, trans. Jackie Smith (New York: New Directions, 2020), 23.

About the Author, Participants, and Contributors

E. G. CRICHTON (she/her) is an interdisciplinary artist living in San Francisco. Her work makes use of a range of art strategies and technologies to explore social issues, archives, history and site-specific subject matter, often in collaboration with partners in other disciplines. Supported by numerous grants and awards, Crichton's work has been exhibited in Asia, Australia, Europe and across the United States. One of the founders of *OUT/LOOK National Lesbian and Gay Quarterly*, she cofounded Q+ Public with Jeffrey Escoffier in 2018. Crichton is a professor emerita of art at the University of California Santa Cruz, and served as artist-in-residence at the Gay Lesbian Bisexual Transgender Historical Society from 2008 to 2014.

ELLIOT ANDERSON (he/him) is a media artist, curator, and educator working in augmented reality documentary, installation, digital photography, and interactive media. He is a professor of art at the University of California, Santa Cruz (UCSC), and co-director of the UCSC Social Practice Arts Research Center. Anderson's work has been exhibited and performed both nationally and internationally. He is a member of the curatorial board of the Berkeley Art Center, where in 2019 he curated the exhibition *Queer Technology*. Anderson's recent artwork and research is an augmented reality documentary for the Ringold Alley Leather Memorial in the San Francisco South of Market neighborhood.

DOMINIKA BEDNARSKA (she/her) is a disabled femme queer academic, writer, solo performer, poet, and activist living in the San Francisco Bay Area.

TERRY BERLIER (they/them) is an interdisciplinary artist who investigates the evolution of human interaction with the natural world, as well as queerness. Berlier makes sculptures and multimedia installations that are kinetic and sound-based. Their work has been exhibited in solo and group shows nationally and internationally. They have held residencies at the Kala Art Institute, the Millay Colony for the Artists, and Lademoen Kunstnerverksteder (LKV) in Norway and have received grants from the California Council for Humanities and the Center for Cultural Innovation. Berlier's work is published in the books *Seeing Gertrude Stein: Five Stories* and *Slant Step Book: The Mysterious Object and the Artworks It Inspired*. Berlier is a professor in the Department of Art and Art History at Stanford University.

TROY BOYD (he/him) was born in Meridian, Mississippi. During the civil rights movement, his family moved north to New Haven, Connecticut, where his father worked in a warehouse. Boyd subsequently attended Boston University, then moved to San Francisco. Since the 1980s, he has lived in Berkeley, where he completed his education. Boyd has been working at the central office of the California Nurses Association since 2013.

TAMMY RAE CARLAND (she/her) is an artist who works with photography, experimental video, and small-run publications. She is professor and provost of academic affairs at California College of the Arts. Her work has been screened and exhibited in galleries and museums internationally, and her photographs have been published in numerous books, including *The Passionate Camera: Photography and Bodies of Desire* and *Lesbian Art in America*. In the 1990s, Carland independently produced a series of influential fanzines, including *I [Heart] Amy Carter*. From 1997 to 2005, she co-ran Mr. Lady Records and Videos, an independent record label and video art distribution company that was dedicated to the production and distribution of queer and feminist culture. She is represented by Silverman Gallery in San Francisco.

LUCIANO CHESSA (he/him) is an experimental composer, musicologist, and performance and visual installation artist from Sassari, Italy. Currently residing in the San Francisco Bay Area again after a two-year sojourn in New York, he composes original works, which he sometimes conducts or at other times plays on a piano, organ, musical saw, or Vietnamese dan bau.

LAUREN CRUX (she/her) is an interdisciplinary artist who works in photography, video, sound, movement, poetry, and text, with a concentration in performance monologues. She has written and performed six full-length solo works, including *My Lunch with Sophia Loren, and Other Stories*, *THREE: A Risky, Irreverent and Curious Look at the Things That Keep Us Awake at Night*, and *On Being Cool, and Other Digressions*. She has performed in Los Angeles at Highways, Los Angeles Contemporary Exhibitions (LACE), and the University of California, Los Angeles, and in the San Francisco Bay area at the Marsh, Luna Sea, Z Space Theatre, Venue 9, and the Julia Morgan Center for the Arts, among others. Crux has also co-created and performed in numerous group and collaborative projects.

BILL DOMONKOS (he/him), a filmmaker who relocated from Oakland, California, to Detroit, creates award-winning experimental films with original soundtracks. His process includes scouring public domain film archives to craft montages that mingle with his original animations. He writes: "Using digital technology, I experiment with combining, altering, editing and reassembling special effects and animations. I am interested in the poetics of time and space, in renewing and transforming materials, experiences, and ideas through the elusive, dreamlike quality of cinema." Domonkos has also created animated GIFs and projections for live performance, video games, and a new immersive virtual reality (VR) music video in collaboration with the band the Residents.

MIKI YAMADA FOSTER (she/her/they/them) is a queer mixed-race multimedia artist working in sound, video, physical technologies, and installation. A skilled facilitator and educator for over fourteen years, she currently works as a data and systems analyst for a labor union and is the co-founder of xcoven/✦✦coven. Yamada Foster has shown work and built creative partnerships with arts and new media organizations, spaces, collectives, and projects in the United States and internationally, including Eyebeam Art and Technology, the Berkeley Art Museum, Radical Networks, the Queer Arts Festival, the Hologram, the MIX Experimental Film Festival, JACK Arts, CultureHub, the Global Action Project, the Wing Luke Museum of the Asian Pacific American Experience, and the Poetry Project.

JAMIL HELLU (he/him) earned his master of fine arts in art practice from Stanford University in 2010. He is the recipient of the San Francisco Arts Commission's Individual Artist Grant, a Zellerbach Family Foundation Community Arts Grant, a Fleishhacker Foundation Eureka Fellowship Award, the Kala Art Institute Fellowship, a residency at Recology San Francisco, a graduate fellowship at Headlands Center for the Arts, and the Cité Internationale des Arts residency in Paris. He has had solo exhibitions at SF Camerawork, the SFO Museum at San Francisco International Airport, Berkeley Art Center, and Les Mots à la Bouche in Paris, among others.

DORIAN KATZ (she/her), an artist who draws no line between the innocent and truly perverse, currently works in graphic novel panels under the pen name Poppers-the-Pony. Katz cofounded the dyke erotica collective Dirty Ink. She curates and shows work in the National Queer Arts Festival, the Center for Sex and Culture, the Exiles (a women's sadomasochism [SM] organization), and SFinX. She has had solo exhibitions at Climate Project Space, Glama-Rama, and the Jon Sims Center. Her drawings are published in *The Human Pony*, *Morbid Curiosity*, and *Salome's Modernity: Oscar Wilde and the Aesthetics of Transgression*. She received a master of fine arts from Stanford University in 2011 and is an art restoration specialist at Art Recovery Technologies (ART).

JONATHAN D. KATZ (he/him) is an art historian, curator, and queer activist. Associate professor of practice in art history and interim director of the Program in Gender, Sexuality, and Women's Studies at the University of Pennsylvania, Katz is a pioneering figure in the development of queer art history and author of a number of books and articles. He curated the first major queer museum exhibition in the

United States, *Hide/Seek: Difference and Desire in American Portraiture* at the Smithsonian National Portrait Gallery, which won several best exhibition and book awards. The first American academic to be tenured in what was then called lesbian and gay studies at City College of San Francisco, Katz was also founding director of Yale University's lesbian and gay studies program. He founded the Queer Caucus for Art of the College Art Association; co-founded Queer Nation, San Francisco; and co-founded the Gay and Lesbian Town Meeting in Chicago. Katz is president emeritus of the Leslie-Lohman Museum for queer art in New York.

NOMY LAMM (she/her/they/them) is a musician, illustrator, voice teacher, creative coach, and Kohenet/Hebrew priest-ess. Lamm is the creative director of Sins Invalid, a disability justice-based performance project, and sings cosmic power ballads for the rise of the matriarchy in a band called the Beauty. Lamm teaches online "sacred fragments" voice classes and creates ritual tools for embodied Jewish feminist practice, including the *Olam haBa 5781 Hebrew Calendar*, with Rebekah Erev, and the *Haggadeck*, with Taya Shere. They live in Olympia, Washington, on occupied Squaxin/Nisqually/Chehalis land with their partner, Lisa, and their animal companions, Dandelion, Momma, Calendula, and Chanukah. (www.nomyteaches.com)

TIRZA TRUE LATIMER (she/her) is professor emerita in the history of art and visual culture at California College of the Arts. Her scholarship investigates visual culture and visual politics from queer feminist perspectives. Latimer's publications include *The Modern Woman Revisited: Paris between the Wars*, a collective volume co-edited with Whitney Chadwick; *Women Together/Women Apart: Portraits of Lesbian Paris*; *Seeing Gertrude Stein: Five Stories*, co-authored with Wanda M. Corn; and *Eccentric Modernisms: Making Differences in the History of American Art.* Her most recent exhibition, *Other Points of View*, was held at the Leslie-Lohman Museum in New York in 2020.

MAYA MANVI (they/them) is a genderqueer artist and educator of South Indian and Latine Diasporas whose practice functions as an ecology of objects, installations, writing, film, and teaching. They hold an MFA in Sculpture from Yale University, and a BFA from UC Santa Cruz. They have held teaching positions at Caldwell University, UC Santa Cruz, Mission High School, and have been a visiting critic at a variety of other academic institutions. Since last Spring, Maya has been working with SFMOMA's Teacher Advisory Group to design innovative decolonized arts curriculum based on the permanent collections and exhibitions. Currently, they serve as the Manager of Educator Engagement at SFMOMA. They have exhibited work in both solo and collaborative capacities in Los Angeles, New York, San Francisco, Berlin, Prague, and Athens.

BARBARA MCBANE (she/her) is a freelance writer, scholar, artist, and filmmaker. She is the former head of critical studies at the Pont-Aven School of Contemporary Art in France. Her scholarly interests center on film sound studies, especially their intersections with questions of race, sexuality, and histories of feminism. Her essays have appeared in film anthologies, exhibition catalogs, the journals *Film Quarterly*, *Art Journal*, and *Film History*, and elsewhere. She has taught gender studies, queer theory, film studies and production, and art-related courses for the University of California at the Santa Cruz, Davis, and Los Angeles campuses and in Ireland and France. For twenty-five years, McBane worked as an award-winning feature-film sound editor and designer on a wide range of projects.

CAMILLE NORTON (she/her) recently published a book of poetry titled *A Folio for the Dark*. Her book *Corruption* was a National Poetry Series winner. Other honors include the Grolier Poetry Prize, an award from the National Endowment for the Humanities, and residencies at the MacDowell Colony, the Ucross Foundation, Ragdale, and the Virginia Center for the Creative Arts. She is a professor of English at University of the Pacific in Stockton, California.

PENSKE (they/them), formerly known as Gabriella Ripley-Phipps, is a queer, ecosexual, polyamorous artist, organizer, friend, witch, astrologer, and teacher. Penske is embedded in a community of witches, radicals, community organizers, parents, and kids in Santa Cruz, California. They spend their time dreaming about interdependence, integrating intergenerational healing and performance, and exploring and playing in nature with kids, dogs, and adults. They study and practice astrology and astronomy. They go to therapy and work in the recovery program of Adult Children of Alcoholics.

ELISSA PERRY (any pronouns used with respect) coedited the collection *Everything Indicates: Bay Bridge Poems and Portraits*. She works with movements to advance equity and liberation as codirector of Change Elemental, an organization dedicated to helping foster system-level change and "deep equity" on issues such as immigration rights, economic development, racial justice, climate justice, and reproductive rights. Perry also teaches in the Master of Arts in Leadership Program at Saint Mary's College, where she helped establish a concentration in social justice.

LAURA RIFKIN (she/her) is the creative catalyst of Fabled Asp—Fabulous/Activist Bay Area Lesbians with Disabilities: A Storytelling Project (www.fabledasp.com). She also co-founded the first disabled women's theater group, Wry Crips Disabled Women's Reader's Theater, in the 1980s and was an early member of AXIS Dance Company in 1990. Rifkin was co-founder of Special Needs Services for Gay Pride in the 1980s and the women's wheelchair basketball team Bay Area Pirates. She is associate producer of *The Way Home*, a film about women, race, and ethnicity. In Rifkin's art, she makes use of scraps to make meaning of the torn and discarded pieces of life.

TINA TAKEMOTO (they/them) is an artist and filmmaker exploring hidden dimensions of same-sex intimacy in Asian American history. Takemoto manipulates archival and found footage through performance and labor-intensive processes of painting, scratching, and lifting 35 mm/16 mm emulsion. By engaging tactile dimensions of the archive, Takemoto conjures up immersive queer historical fantasies. Takemoto has exhibited widely and received grants from Art Matters, ArtPlace, the Fleishhacker Foundation, and the San Francisco Arts Commission. Takemoto was awarded Grand Jury Prize for Best Experimental Film at Slamdance and Best Experimental Film Jury Award at aGLIFF (All Genders, Lifestyles, and Identities Film Festival). Screenings include 50th Ann Arbor Film Festival, Anthology Film Archive, BFI Flare, CAAMfest (presented by the Center for Asian American Media), Outfest, Queer Forever! (Hanoi), and Xposed Queer Film Festival (Berlin). Takemoto is dean of humanities and sciences at California College of the Arts.

MICHELLE TEA (she/her) is the author of over a dozen books, including the cult classic *Valencia*, the popular how-to *Modern Tarot*, and the essay collection *Against Memoir*, winner of the PEN/Diamonstein-Spielvogel Award for the Art of the Essay.

CHRIS E. VARGAS (he/him) is a video maker and interdisciplinary artist currently based in Bellingham, Washington. His work deploys humor and performance in conjunction with mainstream idioms to explore the complex ways that queer and trans people negotiate space within historical and institutional memory and popular culture. He is a recipient of a 2016 Creative Capital award and a 2020 John S. Guggenheim fellowship. In collaboration with Greg Youmans, he made the web-based trans/cisgender sitcom *Falling in Love . . . with Chris and Greg*. With Eric Stanley, Vargas co-directed the movie *Homotopia* and its feature-length sequel *Criminal Queers*. Vargas is executive director of the Museum of Transgender Hirstory & Art (MOTHA).

Index